The Development of the Violent Mind

# THE MIND OF THE DEVIL

The Cases of Arthur Gary Bishop and Westley Allan Dodd

Al Carlisle, Ph.D.

Encino, California

# The Mind of the Devil:
## The Cases of Arthur Gary Bishop and Westley Allan Dodd

### Book 2 in The Development of The Violent Mind Series

Copyright © 2015 Dr. Al Carlisle, Ph.D.

All rights reserved. No part of this book may be reproduced by any means without the written permission of the author or publisher, except for short passages used in critical reviews.

Edited by Steven W. Booth

**Published by:**
Genius Book Publishing
PO Box 17752
Encino, CA 91416
www.GeniusBookPublishing.com

Follow us on Twitter: @GeniusBooks
Like us on Facebook: GeniusPublishing

ISBN: 978-0-9904566-7-4

# Table of Contents

Editor's Note .................................................................. vi
Introduction .................................................................... 1

## Part One: The Case of Arthur Gary Bishop ................ 3

Preface ............................................................................ 5
Prologue ......................................................................... 8
Chapter 1: Childhood .................................................. 15
Chapter 2: The LDS Mission ...................................... 22
Chapter 3: Returning Home ....................................... 29
Chapter 4: Eric ............................................................. 41
Chapter 5: October 17, 1979
    The Homicide of Alonzo Daniels ........................... 49
Chapter 6: November 9, 1980
    The Homicide of Kim Peterson ............................. 53
Chapter 7: October 20, 1981
    The Homicide of Danny Davis ............................... 62
Chapter 8: June 22, 1983
    The Homicide of Troy Ward .................................. 68

Chapter 9: Summer, 1983
    Matt........................................................................70
Chapter 10: The Last Two Months................................74
Chapter 11: July 14, 1983
    The Homicide of Graeme Cunningham .................79
Chapter 12: The Final Fling ............................................84
Chapter 13: The Confession.............................................91
Chapter 14: Prison and Execution ...................................95
Epilogue............................................................................97

## Part Two: The Case of Westley Allan Dodd............................ 103

Preface............................................................................105
Chapter 1: Washington State Penitentiary ....................110
Chapter 2: Contract with Satan.....................................115
Chapter 3: Early Childhood ..........................................122
Chapter 4: Move to Umatilla.........................................129
Chapter 5: The Smallest and Youngest..........................132
Chapter 6: The Pond .....................................................136
Chapter 7: Turning Point ..............................................143
Chapter 8: Fallout..........................................................150
Chapter 9: Ninth Grade.................................................155
Chapter 10: The Next Step............................................159
Chapter 11: First Arrest..................................................167
Chapter 12: Richie and Sammy.....................................171
Chapter 13: Considering Homicide ..............................174
Chapter 14: Cassie .........................................................190
Chapter 15: David Douglas Park...................................199
Chapter 16: The Plan ....................................................203

Chapter 17: Neer Brothers .................................................207
Chapter 18: Escape from the Park ..............................210
Chapter 19: Lee Islie ....................................................213
Chapter 20: Aftermath of Lee's Death .........................215
Chapter 21: Capture .....................................................219
Appendix A ..................................................................222

## Part Three: A Comparison of Bishop and Dodd ..................... 228

Conclusion ...................................................................238

Acknowledgments .......................................................240

## Editor's Note:

The quotes attributed to Arthur Gary Bishop and Westley Allen Dodd are taken from transcripts of interviews with the author before their executions. These are their words.

# THE MIND
# OF THE DEVIL

# Introduction

I had not planned to write a book on Arthur Bishop or Westley Dodd. After all, who wants to read about people who kill children? Much to my surprise, I found that my research raised the question, could seemingly normal children grow up to become killers?

The initial purpose of my research on these men was to do a psychological analysis on each of them in an attempt to obtain an understanding of their backgrounds and histories as killers. But it became much more.

I have often heard psychologists and laypeople say that we will likely never understand how a person becomes a serial killer. I disagree. In fact, I feel we must if we are ever going to find a way to stop the sexual abuse and murder of children. But it's not only the victims we want to save. We also want to stop our children from transforming themselves into killers.

In each case, I began our interviews with their childhoods and gradually moved through their teenage years and into adulthood. I was able to understand—and hope to explain—the progression that Art Bishop and Wes Dodd went through to go from being a normal child to a killer.

# Part One:
# The Case of Arthur Gary Bishop

# Preface

*Nothing is easier than to denounce the evildoer; nothing is more difficult than to understand him.*

*- Fyodor Dostoevsky -*

Arthur Gary Bishop is dead.

He was executed shortly after midnight on June 9, 1988 for the sexual molestation and murder of five children. He died peacefully, unlike the manner in which he killed his victims. Shortly before midnight he was taken from his holding cell and strapped down on a gurney. A hood was placed over his head and the gurney was wheeled into the death chamber. While members of his family and the press watched from an adjoining room a mixture of drugs was injected into his arms and he gradually went to sleep.

His execution brought an end to a terrifying chapter in Utah's history, which began with the death of a young boy on October 16, 1979 and continued until Bishop was caught by Salt Lake City Police detectives in July of 1983. In less four years he had killed five children and had almost killed at least two more. If he had not been caught, he would certainly have continued.

I was with Art throughout the night of his execution. He was afflicted by guilt. He was not depressed nor was he suicidal. He wanted to talk about God and his religion, and he reiterated that he was satisfied that he would be dead in a few hours. He felt at peace with his decision to die.

He had finally got his wish.

❧

My first contact with Arthur Gary Bishop was a couple of days after he was brought to the Maximum Facility of the Utah State Prison and placed on Death Row. I visited him to offer him services from the prison Psychology Department if and when he felt he needed them. I had no interest in talking to him. A psychologist friend of mine, Dr. Alan Roe, and I had conducted hypnosis interviews for the police on a couple of his homicide cases that he later confessed to and I had become acutely aware of the grief the families were feeling at the loss of their children.

On this initial visit, as I sat across the table from this killer of children, a man I wanted to see dead, I felt disgust and I wanted nothing to do with him.

However, when he openly admitted that he was guilty of killing the kids, my mind began to change. I had worked with sex offenders for several years and it was typical for most of them to deny responsibility for their crimes. Bishop's lawyer wanted him to appeal his death sentences, a process which typically extends the life of a killer for ten years or more, but Bishop had no interest in doing this. He said he wanted the families of his victims to obtain some degree of closure, which he thought could not come as long as he was still alive. He was ready to die for his crimes.

Then he said something that truly piqued my interest. He said that before he died, he wanted to understand how he had become a killer. In his mind, he loved kids. They were his only friends. He couldn't understand how he could end the life of people he cared about so much. Even more, he couldn't understand how, following the homicide of his first victim, he could go on killing other children. Being a psychologist, I wanted to understand how it all happened as much as he did. I met with him three times a month after that. He gave me volumes of biographical history to help find the answer.

# Prologue

**October 16, 1979.** Four-year-old Alonzo Daniels was playing on the lawn in front of his apartment complex while his mother was upstairs fixing lunch. In those days, parents didn't worry about strangers wandering off with their children. She checked on him periodically to make sure he hadn't wandered off and to make sure everything was all right. Sometime between noon and 1:00 p.m., when she went to the window to have him come in and eat, he was not there. She walked down the steps to the front of the complex, but still no Alonzo. She called out to him. There was no answer.

She began to get nervous but she thought that he might have seen another little boy in one of the other apartments and had gone to play with him. She checked with her neighbors in the other apartments but no one had seen him. She called frantically for little Alonzo as she ran quickly around the complex but there was still no sign of her child. She returned to her apartment and called the police. They came and made an attempt to find the boy but to no avail. She would never see him alive again.

Almost four years later, on July 14, 1983, a Thursday evening, thirteen year old Graeme Cunningham was at home with his mother. About 8:30 in the evening the phone rang and Graeme answered it. He talked to someone for a few moments and hung up the phone. He told his mother that he had to go out but he would be back shortly. He didn't tell her who was on the phone or where he was going. He just said he wouldn't be gone for very long.

Later in the evening, when Graeme didn't return, Mrs. Cunningham became concerned and called the police. They said they couldn't do anything about it that night because of his age but if he didn't return by morning, she was to call them again. He didn't return that night and the next morning she again reported him missing. Graeme was scheduled to go on a vacation to California on Saturday morning with a man named Roger Downs and his 13-year old stepson, Jess. When Mrs. Cunningham told Roger and Jess that she didn't know where Graeme was, Jess was willing to forego his trip to help find Graeme but Mrs. Cunningham speculated that Graeme would likely show up later and told Roger and Jess to go ahead with their plans. Jess and Graeme were good friends and both of them had gone on other trips with Roger. The established relationship between Graeme, Jess, and Roger precluded any suspicion in Mrs. Cunningham's mind.

The police were particularly troubled by this boy being missing because there had been a series of disappearances of four other boys in the Salt Lake area in the past four years. In addition to this, there was a case of a little girl named Rachael Runyan who was kidnapped in an area north of Salt Lake City in August, 1982. Her body was found under some branches in a creek. While this death was later found to not be related to the other missing children, the public was very concerned because the killer or killers hadn't yet been apprehended.

༄

When the detectives learned about the connection between Graeme and Downs and his stepson, these two became an initial focus in the investigation. They spoke to Graeme's friends about Roger Downs, and one boy reported that Jess was not his stepson. Jess was just a child who spent a lot of time with Roger. They were unable to interview Roger at this point because he and Jess had left for California. They checked for a criminal history on Roger Downs and discovered that his name was actually Arthur Gary Bishop and he had an arrest record.

When Art and Jess returned from their trip, Detective Don Bell informed Bishop that he knew who he really was and that there was a warrant out for his arrest because he had skipped out on probation. It took only a few hours after his arrest until Arthur Bishop confessed to having killed five boys in Salt Lake City.

Art told Detective Bell, "Actually, in a way I feel good telling you about this, but at the same time I know I'm damning myself to hell for doing it. But I'm glad you caught me. I couldn't stop and I would do it again if I had the chance. I get around little kids and I start shaking and I get nervous."

※

Bishop was prosecuted for the murders of five children:

**October 14, 1979.** Alonzo Daniels, age 4, who vanished while playing in front of the apartment complex he was living in.

**November 9, 1980.** Kim Peterson, age 11, told his parents that he was to meet somebody who was interested in buying his roller skates. He never returned home.

**October 20, 1981.** Danny Davis, age 4, was shopping in a grocery store with his grandfather. He was playing in the toy section when somebody lured him out of the store and he was never seen again.

**June 22, 1983.** Troy Ward, age 6, was standing on a corner waiting for his family to pick him up. It was his sixth birthday and they were going to celebrate the occasion that night. When they arrived, he wasn't there.

**July 14, 1983.** Only a few weeks following the disappearance of Troy Ward, Graeme Cunningham, 13, disappeared just before he was to go on a vacation to California with Roger Downs and Jess. His mother never saw him alive again.

☙

Robert Stott was the lead prosecutor in Art's murder trial. The state was going for the death penalty and in order to get it they had to show that each murder was premeditated. Bishop's lead defense attorney was Carol Nessitt-Sales. The prosecution was able to make their case and on March 27, 1984, Bishop was given five death sentences.

Bishop's attorneys petitioned for a new trial, but the Utah Supreme Court rejected it. His lawyers wanted to continue appealing his case but Art petitioned the court for permission to die for his crimes. His lawyers couldn't ethically allow him to give up until all of his appeals had run out. Carol Nessitt-Sales told Art he would have to fire his defense counsel and hire a new set of attorneys who would be willing to abandon any further appeals. He did so. A new competency hearing on Bishop determined that he was aware of what he was doing in petitioning for an early execution so the judge signed the death warrant for the state to go ahead.

Arthur Gary Bishop was executed by lethal injection just after midnight on June 9, 1988. His spiritual leader, Bishop Geurts, and I spent the evening with Art. I was given Art's "last words" to report to the news media following the execution. In a question and answer segment I indicated to Robert Mims, an AP newsman, "I've seen remorse in him from the beginning. He believes he will be going into the spirit world, which will be more peaceful for him than here. He doesn't believe he's been forgiven of his crimes. He believes he can continue to work on the other side on these problems." Bishop Geurts reported to the same AP newsman, "It's unbelievable how calm and cool he is. Even the guards can't understand it. I've dealt with thousands of inmates in 33 years, and he's the most sorrowful and repentant and remorseful man I've ever seen."

※

If Arthur Bishop was so sorrowful and repentant, why did he kill a child in the first place? And, why did he go on killing other children? It didn't make any sense. Most people felt that he was lying in order to *appear* humble and remorseful, hoping that by doing so, people wouldn't hate him as much. Almost nobody believed his protestations of sorrow.

Art said,

> I can't blame anyone for hating me or finding my actions so utterly disgusting. I had really gone off the deep end. My reasons for killing the boys are shallow, selfish, and satanic. Any thought of the grief I would cause the boys' families or other consequences were quickly banished from my mind; I totally failed to appreciate what I was destroying.

Even after witnessing the grief and pain I've caused, still my innermost thoughts and desires are for evil. The god of pedophilia has captured my heart, and no other desire seems so real, strong, insistent, or pleasurable as this. I know the things I've done are sick and revolting to anyone who's normal; yet inside I fear that I would continue such atrocities if given the opportunity. The compulsion to do so is too strong for me to permanently overcome.

Was he lying?

# Chapter 1

## Childhood

Arthur Gary Bishop was born September 9, 1952. He grew up in the small town of Hinkley, Utah, 140 miles southwest of Salt Lake City. He was the fifth of nine children in the home. His family was not wealthy but they had what they needed.

*What was your mother like?*

>I have fond childhood memories of Mom. She was a fantastic cook and baked some of the best bread, cookies, and cinnamon rolls I have ever tasted. My father worked on the railroad and farmed forty acres of land.

*What was your father like?*

> I don't think he really knew how to emotionally express his love for us. I know that Dad loved me and always has, but in my earlier days I mistook his inability to express love as apathy. As a child, I wished that I could have felt closer to him.

*What do you mean by apathy?*

> Well, he just didn't seem to have time for us. He worked long hours in his job and when he came home there were things he had to do on the farm.

*Did you feel you were deprived of his time and attention?*

> No, not really. I felt loved by my parents. Both sets of grandparents were within walking distance from my house and I spent a lot time with them. My childhood was fairly typical in comparison to other kids in the area. I went fishing for carp in the Sevier River and for trout in lakes and larger streams. I helped haul hay and I occasionally helped my grandfather when he milked the cows.

*Did you have any empathy as a child? That is, did it bother you when you saw an animal or child suffering?*

> Yeah, it did. I watched friends being cruel to birds and to kittens. One evening I watched the movie *Bonnie and Clyde*. The final scene showed Bonnie and Clyde being machine-gunned to death. As the bullets tore into them in this seemingly endless sequence, I clenched my hands as an inner

voice screamed, "Stop it! Stop it!" I was trembling and perspiring when it finally ended.

Art was a passive child. He was sensitive and a loner. He never spoke of having close friends. He took part in activities with other boys but he was a follower standing on the periphery of an activity rather than an active leader who planned things. Initially he had an interest in girls, but this was never as strong as his interest in young boys. On one occasion he and another boy were planning some pranks they could do in class. Art put an eraser above the door in a classroom thinking it would come down on the head of one of the students. His teacher came through the door and the eraser hit her on the head. Art got a severe scolding and left the room crying.

> A girl saw me and started crying because I was, and I thought that she must really care about me. Later that day I approached her and asked if she would be my girlfriend. Her emphatic "NO!" left me feeling rejected and confused.
>
> On another occasion some boys dared me to kiss a girl. During recess I sneaked up to the [same] girl and quickly kissed her on the cheek; the girl shrieked and slapped me. A teacher saw the exchange and soon I received a scolding and a lecture. I accepted the lecture without a word, but I decided I didn't ever want to kiss a girl again.

*You asked her to be your girlfriend? You had an interest in girls?*

> The other boys were interested in girls and I wanted to be like these guys.

*Did you continue to have an interest in girls?*

> No. There was a strong emphasis on being morally clean and how sex with girls before marriage was evil. As strange as it may sound, I was told over and over to not have sex with girls but nobody ever said it would be evil to have sex with boys. I know that sounds weird, but somehow to me having sex with boys wasn't the same as with girls. I didn't have any desire to have sex with boys when I was young, but I did have a desire to see what boys looked like naked.

When he was a junior in high school he got an after school job cleaning boy's side of the gym. He would purposely clean the locker room while the younger boys were showering and dressing so he could see them naked.

*Art, were you ever violent when you were a child or a teenager?*

> I had a temper as a kid and it never completely went away. One day I found a pigeon's nest with baby pigeons in it, and took two of the babies home to raise. After a few weeks I began to receive complaints about the mess the fledglings made in the

shed and about them being a nuisance. In anger, I grabbed the pigeons, wrung their necks and threw them violently against the ground. A few days later I found another bird's nest and deliberately killed all the newly hatched birds in it. Another time, I was bird hunting and shot a bird with my pellet gun. I retrieved the dead bird and began to dissect it. I was fascinated with the deaths and dissection. I felt something akin to sexual pleasure.

*When did you begin to feel a sexual attraction to boys?*

When I was about fourteen years old I became attracted to a seven-year-old boy I saw at the local swimming hole in a river in my town. The boy was with his friends learning to swim. I had a strong desire to sexually touch the boy but I needed an excuse to join them. I began going swimming there and I was eventually able to make friends with the boy because I offered to help teach him how to swim. One day I touched the boy's genitals.

*And what happened?*

The boy pushed me away and I hurried and left the swimming hole. Later on I saw the boy swimming alone and a strong desire to see the boy naked came over me, but I thought the boy would report me. I thought that in order to fondle the boy I must first kill him. I briefly considered how I might do it but I didn't know where to hide the body. When I realized what I was thinking and how wrong it was I left the area and went home.

It surprised Art that he had these thoughts. It didn't seem to frighten him though, because even though he was beginning to become sexually attracted to young boys, this had been only a brief thought and he was able to quickly dismiss it. However, by the age of fifteen, Art realized that he was different from his peers. Some of the kids in school had been teasing him because he was overweight. He wore glasses (they called him "Four Eyes") and he had a mild speech problem. The greatest difference that he detected between himself and the other boys his age, however, was that his sexual interest was towards boys and not girls.

※

In 1970, Art graduated Delta High School with honors. He was third in a class of 103 students. He got his Eagle Scout award and he got a special award in his church because of his religious activity. He received a scholarship for Stevens-Henagar College. During the summer following graduation from high school he worked as a desk clerk in a motel owned by his uncle. In the fall he attended Stevens-Henagar College in Salt Lake, specializing in business and bookkeeping.

> Occasionally I would go to a swimming pool and watch the boys changing in the dressing room. I lived in an apartment where for two months a young boy came to the apartment. I masturbated him. [Soon after,] I was arrested for shoplifting. I

plead guilty and I completed one year's probation. My sexual problem was getting out of hand and this bothered me.

# Chapter 2

## The LDS Mission

Art was a member of the Church of Jesus Christ of Latter-Day Saints (LDS), often referred to as the Mormons. A boy who has been a worthy member of the Church is allowed to go on a two-year mission at his own expense to teach others about the Church.

*Art, you went on an LDS mission, right?*

>Yes, I had taken the seminary [religion] classes in school and I got my Duty to God award in church. In September of 1971 my bishop asked me if I would be interested in going on a mission for the LDS Church.

# The Case of Arthur Gary Bishop

*But you were sexually attracted to boys. How were you able to be religious and be sexually attracted to kids?*

I believed in God and the Church. Other boys were going on missions and my mother hoped I would too. I said I would go, which was partly because I wanted to please my mother. Another reason was because I had engaged in masturbation with another boy several times and my desire for sexual involvement with young boys was getting out of hand. I hoped that by going on a mission it would cure my desire for sex with boys.

*Did it work?*

It did for a while. I wanted to be clean and worthy when I started on my mission so I stopped masturbation several months before I left. My sexual problem frightened me and I was hoping that this would provide the cure I needed to become normal.

*Did you go on your mission because you felt obligated to go? That is, did you feel pressured to serve a two-year mission because you believed it was expected of you?*

No, I wanted to go. Our family wasn't all that religious. My dad was only partially active in the church and he didn't care if I went or not. I believed in God and I felt better when I was in church. I was hoping that if I went on a mission for God that He would give me the power to control my sexual urges.

*Did anything go wrong on your mission?*

> I was assigned to go to the Philippine Islands. I left on my mission in November of 1971. I was 21 years old when I returned in November of 1973. I didn't tell anybody about my sexual problem because I thought I could work it out on my own. However, it was common to see young boys running around naked over there but I found that if I didn't look at them I was able to control those urges. I enjoyed my missionary work and I was able to control my urges for the first year of my mission.

*But what happened?*

> I began to weaken when I kept seeing nude children and I was beginning to long for home. The heat and humidity sapped my energy and I was getting discontented with the missionary work. I wanted to do something new and different.

He learned that the Mission Home was in need of a commissary clerk/bookkeeper. This was his area of expertise and his chosen career for the future. He asked to be considered for the position partly because it offered a higher status than his usual missionary work, and it would get him away from the naked boys he saw running around everywhere.

When the position was given to another missionary, Art felt hurt and depressed. Shortly after this he and his missionary companion were in a home of a family they were attempting to teach. A boy of about nine or ten years old came into the room from having taken a bath. The boy was naked and he sat in front of Art. Art got extremely aroused and that night while taking a shower unintentionally climaxed.

> I felt devastated after having such a long, successful abstinence. I felt defeated and very guilty. I assumed that my repentance had been for naught.

*What do you mean?*

> I had promised God that I would change and that I would stop masturbating. I didn't want to be sexually attracted to boys and I felt I had broken my promise to God. I never totally recovered my confidence back after this incident. I endured numerous "indulge and then repent" cycles and I felt depressed and ashamed most of the time and finally I wrote a letter to the mission president and told him how depressed I felt, and that I wanted to quit my mission and go home.

The next Monday he was called into the mission president's office. Art told him about the masturbation problem he was having. The mission president urged him to stay.

> He reassured me and consoled me. He gave me encouragement to keep fighting and gave me a special blessing. I left his office feeling uplifted and much better. We talked briefly a couple of times

after that. I was moved to a different area of the island and I was made a supervisor over three other missionaries. I felt a new sense of inspiration! I was going to do a good job! I wanted so much to be able to turn it all around and feel constant spirituality. We worked pretty hard, and I kept especially busy with my missionary and group responsibilities.

*Did you tell your mission president that you were sexually attracted to the naked boys you saw running around?*

No. It was too embarrassing to tell him that.

*What would have happened had you told him?*

He might have sent me home.

*But you had already told him that you wanted to go home.*

He encouraged me to stay and complete my mission. It felt so good when he told me that, that I wanted to stay. I had already completed half of my mission and I thought I could control myself enough to make it through another year.

Then I began noticing the naked children more, my sexual impulses were aroused, and I began masturbating a lot. I knew I had opened the door wide open for Satan, but my resistance was weak. These sexual thoughts could not coexist with any feelings of spirituality.

He read his scriptures, said his prayers, and was having success in bringing converts into the church, but he couldn't keep himself from getting sexually aroused when he saw naked boys. He vacillated daily between attending to his sexual cravings and his desire for spirituality. It was only a matter of time before this conflict would wear him down and set him up for another catastrophic event.

> One day I picked up a small boy outside my apartment and momentarily fondled him. I felt immediately disgusted with myself. What would these people think of a Mormon missionary who molested boys? I felt horrible inside. The love I had for these kids was becoming perverted, and I knew I was becoming more evil every day.
>
> I felt unworthy to continue my mission. I didn't want to be sent home in disgrace, so there was only one way out. I bought a large bottle of aspirin and claimed I felt too ill to go out with the other missionaries after a noon break. I thought little of what I was doing or its consequences, I just wanted to escape from the unhappiness and self-disappointment I was experiencing. I swallowed all of the aspirin and laid on my bed.

*It sounds like you were serious about wanting to die.*

> My emotions were mixed. I felt a kind of excitement from an impending release from all my cares, but I felt saddened by what Mom's reaction might be. I didn't leave a note because I didn't know how

to explain. After a few minutes a constant buzzing began in my ears, I felt slightly nauseated, and it seemed harder to breathe. The buzzing got louder, the breathing more difficult, and I was perspiring; yet I felt relaxed and peaceful. The thought, "So this is what it feels like to die," crossed my mind and I felt I was almost there.

*Then what happened?*

All of a sudden I got very nauseous. I threw up in the wastebasket several times and I just laid and rested and nothing happened and I started feeling better. That was a serious suicide attempt. I had been there in that area as a group leader three or four months. I sent a letter to the mission president and I was transferred to another area. I was never able get to the point where I could totally keep my eyes off the kids like I used to.

[After I was reassigned,] I got a new, energetic spiritual companion. Many days were spent in hard work, and I felt good sometimes, but inside I had given up on any sincere attempt to master my sexual desires. I rationalized away the seriousness of my sins, and did what missionary work I could with my diminished spirituality. I had successes, good days, conversions—but it could have been so much more meaningful with a full-hearted effort.

## Chapter 3

### Returning Home

Art completed his mission and he got home just before Thanksgiving in 1973. He gave a homecoming speech in church which impressed his listeners.

> I was really up for that. People afterwards really commented on how good it was. I spent a lot of time preparing it and I put humor in it and I told about the families I had met and had baptized. Many people complimented me whom I was surprised to get a compliment from.

In the eyes of most people in his family, his church and his town, Art had completed a successful mission. People looked up to him. They expressed their respect and admiration, but he didn't feel that he deserved their praise. In his eyes he had failed miserably because he was still sexually attracted to boys. He felt he didn't deserve to be in church on Sundays and the only way he could minimize his guilt was to avoid any place or discussion that generated guilt. At this point in his life, Art had given up on his attempt to change. It wasn't that he couldn't change, it was that he didn't want to try any longer.

> We had a company out there [in the area of Delta, Utah] called Brush Beryllium that dealt in refining metals. I applied with them as a bookkeeper. They didn't have an opening for a bookkeeper but they hired me to be a laborer, cleaning up and anything else they needed. I had a schedule where I worked ten days on and had ten days off so every other weekend I was working Sundays. It was all right because in a way I was tired of so much religion.

*Art, I'm not sure I understand that. When you were on your mission you were deeply involved with your missionary work. You felt so guilty about your sexual problem that you attempted suicide. And now when you get home, you are tired of so much religion? There must be more to it than simply being tired of religion.*

> I believed that I had repented of my sins before I went on my mission and that God had forgiven me. However, I had sinned again with this boy, and

> I realized that I hadn't gotten over being sexually aroused by boys. I had a very a strong desire to molest that boy. If you sin and repent and get forgiven and then sin again, I believe it cancels out having been previously forgiven. When I touched the boy I was guilty of not only this sin, but now also of all of my previous sins. I gave up on my belief that I could change. The urge to molest that boy was so strong I was afraid that I might not ever be able to avoid being attracted by boys.
>
> Another thing that kind of irked me was that people think when you come home from a mission you are like you were an angel out there. They really put the missionaries up on a high pedestal.

One Sunday when Art went to church he was asked at the last minute to teach a Sunday School class of about six teenagers. All he had to do was to go to class and talk about his experiences on his mission. He had had many good ones. However, Art had always felt that he had to be well prepared in order to do a decent job. In this situation, he felt totally unprepared.

> I felt like a total jerk and the lesson didn't go well. I got to the point where on the Sundays that I didn't work and was able to go to church, I didn't go. I had long since quit praying and stuff like that. I didn't feel like I needed it anymore.

*Art, was it that you didn't need religion any longer or had you given up on trying to change? You tried very hard to be spiritual when you were on your mission and now, within a period of only a few weeks, you felt you didn't need God any longer? Did you give up on God or do you believe that God gave up on you?*

> I gave up on God and when I did I believed that God gave up on me. When I was in the mission field I didn't ever think that I would fall away from the Church. I said, Not me. Not ever. This means too much to me. Yet within a matter of three or four months after I got home I was inactive. The sexual urges I had fought all of my life began to re-emerge and they were strong.

With the money Art earned from his work, he bought a motorcycle and started giving rides to young kids. He found himself getting turned on by them and one day he pulled down the pants of one of the boys and touched his gentiles. He apologized and asked the kid not to tell his parents. Art figured that nobody made an issue of it partly because he was a returned missionary and partly because of the respect the people in his small town had for his family.

> I think she [the boy's mother] just didn't know what to do. She never said anything. I think, really, had she said something and this had come out in the open before I was starting to get these strong desires again, I think I could have turned around and stopped. I don't know if I could have ever really completely lost these desires but I think I could

have learned how to control them. That would have been important I think. After that I never went to church again, except maybe once or twice. I felt unworthy to go to it. I had a lot of spiritual training as I was growing up and I had a strong testimony at one time but it seemed like everything went away.

*Why do you think it went away? Was it there in the first place or did you go on your mission simply to please your mother?*

I was religious when I was on my mission. I went partly for my mother and partly to get control over my sexual urges but I had a testimony of the work I was doing and when I was active in the work I felt that God was pleased with me.

*So what made you give it all up?*

When I tried to stop having the desires to molest children, the harder I tried to stop, the stronger those desires became. I got tired of trying to control them so I gave up trying. I didn't have any urges to go out and find children to molest at that point but I accepted the fact that this was who I was.

A dramatic change would now begin to take place in his personality. He made his final separation from his religion and his Deity, and "accepted the fact that this was who I was," there was no longer a strong motivation to overcome his problem. His motivation would be about how to satisfy his urges and not get caught. From this point on, the drive for sex with children never stopped. Initially, the pathology was about what he was doing. The pathology would be who he is. It will become his identity and, the more he gives in to it, the stronger his addiction will become.

However, he grew up with religious beliefs. Will he ever be totally free from them? A killer I knew said, "You can't kill the conscience!" If this is true then Art would likely have pangs of sorrow and guilt intermittently along with his drive for sexual satisfaction with kids.

*Art, how strong were those desires to molest children?*

> I was reading a book the other day where it was talking about psychopaths. It said something to the effect that strange gods call after them and *that* calling is dearer to their heart than anything else. I thought, if that doesn't describe pedophilia, I don't know what does. It's a god and it controls everything you do.

*What do you mean when you say it controls everything you do?*

> I got to the point of being so aroused by boys that I conditioned myself, unknowingly, to *want* to get sexually involved with them. I would masturbate two or three times a day, always picturing young boys, and I would still feel unsatisfied. It's like I just couldn't get enough.

*Is this why there is an escalation in this behavior?*

> Yes. After you reach your climax and you still don't feel satisfied you want to do it again. And

because of this you feel a need to seek something that is more exciting, and for this reason you begin to do things like. . . you just can't look at boys, you feel you have to touch them, and then you may want to fondle them, and you want to take pictures of them so after the boy is gone you can still enjoy getting turned on by looking at the pictures. And, it escalates. What was once very shocking—and actually to the normal mind would be sickening—the fact that it is wrong adds more excitement to it. At this point you become more hardened. It's a gradual process but as you do more and more wicked things, you want to do even more wicked things.

Art needed help but he was unwilling to divulge his hidden passion for sexual involvement with children. He had given up on God because God hadn't taken this curse from him. He felt guilty when he went to church, so he gave that up. The only way he could deal with God and religion was to put them out of his life. He told me that he had a strong grasp of the scriptures when he was on his mission and he could elucidate on any religious topic. He put his scriptures away so he wouldn't have to look at them. Instead, he fed his sexual passion every day because the pleasure was immediate.

In July, 1974, Art went to Stevens-Henagar College in Ogden for a year and lived with a relative. In July 1975, after he graduated, he got his first full time job. It was as a bookkeeper at a car dealership in Salt Lake City. An aunt in Salt Lake invited him to stay with her and her family until he could save up enough money to get his own place. He accepted the offer, partly because he needed to save up for his own place and partly because he was lonely and he didn't want to be alone.

His aunt had four boys whose ages ranged from about four to fourteen and once again he felt he had some friends he could do things with. He again was with a family. "I enjoyed their company and spent time with them going to movies, hiking, camping, or skiing."

However, he also found himself getting aroused by his cousins. He began sneaking into their rooms at night to try to fondle them while they were asleep. He got caught a couple of times by the boys but they didn't tell their parents. He came across some pornographic literature that interested him and he began actively seeking more of it. His sexual appetite was getting out of hand.

> I had lived here 7 or 8 months and I was ashamed and disgusted with myself, so I moved from my aunt's house because of my guilt feelings, to avoid potential trouble, and to possibly get more freedom in a place of my own.

He couldn't stop himself from desiring the boys and he was afraid that sooner or later one of them would tell on him so, as soon as he had the money, he moved out of his aunt's home into an apartment in Midvale, Utah. He was working and began to steal money from work in amounts of $50 to $100 and used that money to proposition boys to allow him to take nude pictures of them. "I was lonely and I began to seek out boys to try to appease that loneliness." He propositioned a boy in a restroom of a swimming pool and the boy went out and told the lifeguard who called the police, but he left before they could catch him. He propositioned another boy in his neighborhood who then told his parents and they called the police. In both cases he was able to avoid being arrested.

One Saturday Art was invited over to his aunt's place for a family barbeque. Later in the evening when the youngest child was taking a bath, Art went in to keep him company and he fondled the boy in the tub while he talked to him. Art was unaware that the bathroom window was open and members of the family were outside on the patio. His aunt overheard him talking to her son and she came inside to see what was going on. When she saw Art kneeling by the tub next to her son, who was four or five years old, she suspected what he was doing.

She didn't say anything at that point but she talked to her other sons who said Art would come into their bedroom at night and fondle them. The aunt reported it to Art's older sister who confided in a brother, and the two of them came to his Midvale apartment to confront him about it. He opened up to them and told them of his desires for children. Since he seemed honest with them, they said they wouldn't call the police if he would get professional help. Art agreed.

He saw a psychologist a few times and told him of his sexual interest in boys (but didn't clarify that he meant prepubescent children). Some suggestions were made, including encouragement to get involved in outside interests to give his life more meaning. Art saw him only a few times and then stopped going to therapy.

> As a pedophile you don't seek help voluntarily. I had periods of time when I was totally disgusted with myself. I was despondent and I hated what I was doing and during these periods of time I would make an effort to stop. You think, hey, I'm going to quit this. I'm going to see somebody and get some help. But when those sexual urges come back, you lose your desire to give them up.

*But you knew that sooner or later you would get caught and you would be in a lot of trouble. Wasn't there something you could do to stop?*

> This is the only enjoyment I get. I'm not going to voluntarily see a therapist. Had I not been forced to seek help I probably wouldn't have, and as soon as I could drop it, I did. so if somebody knows someone with a problem like mine who is seeing a therapist they better make sure he keeps seeing him. Even with counseling, once you have these desires it's such a learned behavior, learned over so many times, and reinforced so many hundreds of times, you may like to change but you just plain don't know how anymore. That's what's so frustrat-

ing. You know you are like this and people hate you for being this way, but what can you do about it? You feel virtually helpless.

*What do you mean by helpless?*

Well, in my case, boy sex became my god and the desire to please that god was greater in my heart than any other desire because it was more realistic. There was more compulsion involved with it, more pleasure involved than in any other thing I've known. And so, as much as I may hate myself at times for feeling this way—and a lot times, I wish I could live a normal life—at the same time when the sexual urges arise, that god takes over and I'll do my best to please him.

*What do you mean by more realistic?*

Pleasing [this] god may give you a more peaceful life and you will get rewards in heaven but that wouldn't satisfy my sexual desires here on earth.

*As you look back now, do you think there was anything that could have been done?*

I think so. Had it been done earlier, like right after my mission. It wasn't that strongly ingrained in me yet. It was there and maybe I would still have these latent desires, but I think had I got the proper training and counseling maybe I would have the desires but I would not act them out. And that would have been the key.

*But when you did go to counseling, you were still not willing to tell your therapist about your sexual desire for children. Wasn't that an opportunity to open up and begin working on the problem?*

>It was almost too late by then. Besides, it was too embarrassing to tell someone that I got aroused by children. I had no romantic interest in girls. Young boys were my only enjoyment. I didn't want to give that up.

After a few months he moved to another location. This would be a consistent pattern from here forward.

>I was too scared to actually seek out boys and take the risks I did before. My embezzling at my work increased. I stole enough money to completely pay off my student loan, and then to buy a new Honda 550cc motorcycle. Eventually I had stolen enough to buy a new 4wd GMC pickup. In retrospect, I can see how my decreased risks in the pursuit of pedophilia increased the risks I took in embezzling. Did I need excitement so bad?

# Chapter 4

## Eric

Art became acquainted with a boy named Eric who he attempted to fondle and found the boy to be receptive to it. His sister and brother were familiar with this boy and his mother so they were concerned about Art's relationship with the boy. In the case of Westley Dodd, he had come to love two boys, which was a huge part of his downfall. In much the same manner as Dodd did with his two boys, Art got very close to Eric. This was to become a serious problem for him. Art was very lonely. He needed a companion, not only for sexual gratification but to have someone to do things with. Art had no idea how to relate to adults, so that left only kids.

He was a constant turn on to me, to put it bluntly. I decided I wanted him for me and so I told my sister that we were working on a project as part of my therapy where I was given some medicine and then put in a position where I could be turned on by a boy. I told her that if I acted out on that boy, this medication in my system would cause a reaction where I would get violently ill. She believed me. I really hadn't lied to her very much before this time. For a long time this worked and I was able to be sexually involved with this boy. At this point I knew I was really doing things wrong and I knew people would hate me for it, yet the compulsion to do it was so strong I didn't want to stop.

*How would you feel after one of these sexual engagements with this boy?*

I never felt totally right and sometimes it would bother me a lot more than at other times. But this is when I began learning to block out these feelings.

*Was it guilt that you were learning to block out?*

Yes, and this was what eventually led me to be able to kill without really feeling a lot of pain. You learn to build a shell around some of these emotions. Otherwise, I think a person would realize how sick he is becoming. I would read about other people doing things like this and it would justify me doing it.

# The Case of Arthur Gary Bishop

But it wasn't all bad. I did a lot of good things for these boys. It may not have excused the evil I was doing to them but to me at the time it seemed like I may be doing bad things to them but I was doing good things as well. I would give them gifts like buying a boy an expensive camera, I bought him a dirt bike, a shotgun, stereo, a lot of records and tapes, and this was just to keep him happy.

*You're talking about Eric, right?*

Yeah.

*Where did you get the money for these gifts?*

The way I got the money was embezzling. We had tons of fun and all it would cost him is to let us masturbate together.

*Did buying things for him seem to appease the guilt as well as entice the boy to do sexual things with you?*

Yeah, a lot.

*Were you in love with Eric?*

Yeah. I would get jealous if he showed interest in other boys. I wrote a company check for $6,000 and used it as a down payment on a house in Sandy. The house was for Eric as much as for me. I wanted to do things to please him, and my own needs were secondary to his.

I really liked the house in Sandy, but more importantly, Eric did. I bought a queen-sized waterbed for Eric and me to sleep on. I bought a pretty expensive fur-like bedspread to take pictures of Eric on because it made him very sexy. I got an expensive camera and made my own darkroom to develop film in.

A time came while Art was living in Midvale, Utah, and his brother was working in Salt Lake, that Art allowed his brother to temporarily live with him while he looked for a job. One day his brother asked Art if he had any magazines he could read. Art told him to go look in a drawer in his dresser where he kept his magazines. His brother opened the wrong drawer and saw nude pictures of boys. One of them was of his sister's boy. When the brother reported it to their sister, they were incensed because Art had been lying to them all this time about his supposed therapy. For his sister, that was the last straw.

> I got a letter from my sister saying I don't want to see you again. I don't want to consider you my brother. If ever [you are] down home visiting Mom and you see my car there in the driveway, don't stop. If we're down visiting her and we see your car, we won't stop. I don't want to see you again.

They threatened to report him to the police if he didn't stop spending time with kids. Trouble was also brewing in the company where he was employed. One morning when Art went to work, his boss informed him that he and the owner of the company had got into and argument and that he was going to quit and go to work for another company. Art said he would quit as well, which outwardly appeared to be an act of loyalty. However, Art was quitting because he had embezzled a large amount of money from the company to pay his rent, for gifts for Eric and for daily living.

> I couldn't quit embezzling, so I determined that I should quit the job. When I left, I took many of the accounting records with me. When the dam breaks on someone's moral norms and taboos, the break is abrupt and lets loose a flood of misbehaviors that feed on themselves and the problem grows in exponential proportions.

It had been less than five years since he had gotten home from his mission. He had gone to college to finish his education and he was skilled as a bookkeeper. He had no problem obtaining a new job and his employers trusted him. He had given up his religion and he had to move away from his hometown and from his friends, neighbors and family. He had alienated family members who had tried to help him. He was sexually involved with kids and couldn't give it up.

> In 1978, I embezzled where I was working. I got caught and arrested. I went to trial in 1978 and I went to a halfway house. I didn't have a record prior to that so the judge put me on probation and restitution. I embezzled $47,000, I believe. I was paying $100 a month restitution. One of the stip-

ulations was that I see a psychologist until he was satisfied that I got the treatment I needed. I saw Dr. Cory Hammond. We talked mostly about criminal behavior, like why I needed to steal. He had me read some books and he'd have me discuss a chapter each session regarding what I thought was important as it applied to me. He was very good. I quite liked him.

Being in the halfway house was terrifying for Art. Some of the inmates he came in contact with looked mean and tough and he was fearful of what they might do to him if they were aware that he was molesting children. Also, he felt empty and alone without children in his life. He hated not having his freedom. He told himself that he would never get locked up again.

Dr. Hammond used a number of therapy techniques including bringing in a female therapist when Art said he wasn't interested in girls or men. Art was told he was free to talk about dating or sex or any other topic of his choosing with this female therapist. Art said he enjoyed talking to her. He enjoyed the openness because he felt he was learning new things. Art was getting good therapy for the problems he was willing to talk about. The only problem with the therapy was that Art had never been arrested for a sexual assault on a minor and he wasn't about to tell Dr. Hammond about his attraction to children. The only official information about his criminal behavior was that he embezzled.

After being released from the halfway house he lived in an apartment on the northeast side of Salt Lake, an area generally referred to as The Avenues. He continued to see Eric in secret but then the relationship came to an end, because Art's primary problem was not the sex, but the loneliness. He didn't have anyone else in his life but boys and he equated companionship with sex. He had no one now so he joined the Big Brother program and was assigned a Little Brother. The boy's mother had requested an LDS Big Brother because she wanted her son to go on an LDS mission. Art was happy with this and he began acquainting the boy with what it is like to be a missionary. However, the program learned that Art had an arrest record and he was dropped.

During this time he also met a boy named Jess, a neighborhood boy who was about ten years old. Jess's father passed away and Jess began spending a lot of his spare time with Art. They engaged in some sexual activities and Art would give him gifts. Art was replacing Eric with Jess.

> I was unhappy with life. I was hating myself because I couldn't control my sexual acts. I justified my actions of both sex and theft by saying to myself that I would commit suicide before I would go to prison.

Art was now in a very precarious position in his life. He had an arrest record and he was terrified about the police finding out about his sexual activities with children.

He didn't like what he had become but he had made the decision that he couldn't change. Art was about to make a decision that would catastrophically alter his life.

# Chapter 5

### October 17, 1979
### The Homicide of Alonzo Daniels

Art got another job as a bookkeeper at a steel company but he wasn't making enough money to make his restitution payments and still have money to entice kids to engage in sexual activities with him. He would either have to give up bribing kids for sexual activities or he would have to find a way to get out from under his restitution payments. He chose the latter. He stopped going to therapy. He moved to a new location and didn't inform his probation officer about it. There was now a warrant out for his arrest.

*Tell me about your first victim. You loved boys and you relied on them to appease your loneliness. Relationships with boys were your main interest. How did you make the choice to kill a child?*

> The first one I killed? I had never met him before that day. By the time I met this boy there were a lot of things going on in my mind. I had been in a halfway house. I heard about things that were done to child molesters in prison. They said that other inmates would beat you up and knife you and rape you. One guy said the inmates will use you for sex. I got a definite fear of coming to prison as a child molester. I made this mental decision that rather than ever going to prison I would die first. I would commit suicide.
>
> Also, I was very disgusted with myself and I went to the Church and I requested that I be excommunicated. I knew what I was doing was wrong. Here I am molesting all these boys and if I am doing this, is it going to hurt to steal money? I kind of justified my actions that way. It's like a sex sin is so bad that nothing else is so bad in comparison to it.

*You asked to be excommunicated?*

> Yeah, I did. It was in September, 1979.

*What was the purpose of that?*

> I believe that God judges you according to your knowledge and understanding. I get blessings if I'm

active in the Church, but there are responsibilities as well. I thought that if I was no longer a member of the Church, God may not judge me as harshly.

*Did you tell the Church authorities about you sexual activities with boys?*

No, I said I was being immoral with a girl.

*So, how did the homicide come about?*

I lived in an apartment close to where I was working and I would come home to eat lunch at noon and return to work about 1:00 pm. One day when I came home for lunch I saw a young boy playing outside. I was very attracted to this boy and I invited him into my apartment to play with some toys.

While the boy, Alonzo Daniels, was playing, Art became aroused and attempted to fondle him. Alonzo began to cry. Art was fearful of the boy reporting it to his mother, who would likely report it to the police. Art couldn't let that happen so he hit Alonzo over the head with a hammer and killed him. Art said that when he raised the hammer to hit the boy, his arm froze in place and he heard something inside him yelling, "NO!!!" When he hit the boy he felt something pull out of him and motioned to his chest when he said this. He felt it was something akin to a conscience.

He called work and said he wouldn't be coming back that day because he wasn't feeling well. He put the boy's body in a box and carried it out to his car. As he passed

Alonzo's apartment he could hear Alonzo's mother frantically calling around to see if anybody had seen her son. He buried the boy in the Cedar Fort area south of Salt Lake City. That night he could hear the boy's mother screaming in anguish. He had nightmares and he felt haunted by the boy.

> For a few days after this I was in shock. I had an urgent feeling of impending disaster. I slept uneasily at night. I dreamed of that day over and over. I was afraid to be alone and afraid of the dark. Sometimes I felt distant from reality and had a hard time concentrating.
>
> I couldn't stand to stay any longer in the apartment so I moved back to the Avenues in Salt Lake. I began to have nightmares less and less, and life began to calm down. I felt ashamed of what I had done and wished to erase this guilt from my life. I got a new identity and quit my job at the steel company after embezzling money to support me.

## Chapter 6

### November 9, 1980
### The Homicide of Kim Peterson

Arthur Bishop was now going under the name of Lynn Jones. He had found a way to obtain a false social security card and driver's license to support this new name. He didn't have a desire to continue killing children but now that he had actually killed one child he didn't have any strong reservations against doing it again. He lived in the Avenues for a short while and then moved again. He had a warrant out for his arrest but decided that as long as he wasn't picked up by the police he would be safe staying in the Salt Lake area.

I moved to a small, out-of-the way house on south State Street. I was unemployed for a while and spent my time obtaining a driver's license and a social security number. Finally I was able to get a job at a large ski organization. Jess continued to come over and he let me take pictures of him when I pressured him. It had been about a year since my incident with Alonzo, but the sexual urgings were still there, along with a despair of knowing I had cut myself off from my family. The only relief I could find was a temporary sexual one and I would constantly seek erotic sights to stimulate me. Young boys seen walking around or on TV would excite me, and numerous trips were made to the bookstores for picture books, and to swimming pool dressing rooms.

One day when I was with Jess, a young boy of 13, Kim Peterson, began getting friendly with Jess, and after a while bummed a ride to his home from us. He had wanted to sell some roller skates, and I told him I would call him the next day and let him know what I decided. He was very outgoing and I felt that he would not be embarrassed about having his picture taken.

I called him the next day and arranged to meet him. Once we met I told him I wasn't interested in his skates, but offered to give him some money if he would go hunting with me. He agreed and I took him to a hunting area and after a lot of coaxing he agreed to let me take a picture of his genitals on the condition I would let him take one of me.

> I agreed. The pictures were taken. We finished and were walking back to the car when he stated that he wanted me to meet him at a game arcade in Salt Lake and give him money every week.

Art didn't like the thought that Kim was blackmailing him. "My thought was I've already killed. Will I be damned any more for two lives?" As Kim was walking away from him, Art shot him in the back. Kim died moments later. When he first took Kim out to the hunting area, he sensed he was going to end up killing him but now that he had actually done so he was upset with himself. He walked around for a few minutes and then hid the body behind some bushes. He realized he hadn't brought a shovel so he drove back to Salt Lake to get one. He returned and buried the boy. He was still very upset and vomited until he got the dry heaves. He hated himself and put the muzzle of his pistol in his mouth but couldn't pull the trigger. The thought of suicide was brief, impulsive, and superficial. It wasn't until after killing Graeme Cunningham several years later that he would become more intent on following through with a plan to take his own life.

> Many of the same feelings were with me at Kim's murder as were with me at Alonzo's death. I knew I had blown it but the feeling was as if I wasn't actually personally involved in the action. Afterwards I went through a period of emptiness for a while and the nightmares came again.

Art continued his relationship with Jess but he became jealous of him. He was angry at himself for being so attached to Jess and over the fact that he actually had very little control over him. Jess could come and go as he wanted and the only way Art was able to keep him around was to offer gifts and activities such as camping and skiing and vacations. Art needed Jess and he dreaded the time that Jess would leave him for other friends and girlfriends.

Jess enjoyed his relationship with Art but much of it was because his mother was poor, he had lost his father, and Art had become a substitute father showering him with attention. Jess was not sexually attracted to Art and he only tolerated the sexual activities. There are no indications that he was aware of the homicides.

> I had become very fond of Jess, and loved him as much as I had ever loved anyone. He was my close friend, a companion who eased my loneliness and someone with whom I could go out and have fun. I often felt like a father to him and wished that he could be my son permanently. I gave him numerous gifts, many of them quite expensive.
>
> Though I loved Jess, I also hated him at times. He represented a personal temptation including sick sexual deviancy which served as a constant reminder that I was not normal. I feared him growing up and leaving me alone. Many, many times I was mentally cruel to him. I would purposely start

arguments, or hurt him with unkind remarks, or make fun of him, gloating inwardly if he burst into tears or stamped out of the house in anger. It was like I wanted to punish myself by making him leave me.

I have to admit something further about my cruelty. Seeing Jess angry or crying or hurting made me feel wanted and needed. I was so insanely jealous of Jess that I could hardly let him develop relationships with others without feeling jealous and slighted. A few times I begrudged the love he showed his own mother. Some of Jess's friends provided opportunities for sex for me, but if I felt that their relationships with Jess were taking precedence over my own fragile relationship, then I became frustratingly jealous and behaved childishly by being mean and ornery. It hurt my feelings of worth if Jess paid too much attention to his friends, family, or pets. I was like a child who needed constant hugs of attention and reassurance.

Art was seriously beginning to deteriorate. He hated himself for his obsessive dependence on Jess and other children. He couldn't stand being alone. He was afraid of the dark and when he would lock up the building at work at night following his janitorial duties at the steel company he would drive his car over to the door and shine his lights on the lock so he wouldn't have his back to the dark. He had always had a problem with fear. When he was a child, the sheets on his bed had a floral pattern that reminded him of giant spiders, and the wind blowing the limbs of the tree outside his window looked like scary monkeys. When he did his janitorial work at night, the creaking sounds from the building sounded as if someone was walking around above him. He brought a radio to drown out those sounds.

He enjoyed reading Steven King novels because, "Steven King would get my imagination going and I couldn't shut it down." But he wouldn't read King's books at night. He primarily enjoyed stories and movies with kids in them because he could identify with them. "To me, any movie that has a little boy in it is a lot nicer because I can put myself in that boy's place and enjoy it. A lot of people who see a sexy woman in a scene find it interesting. I don't." When I asked him what age he would pick to be if he could remain at one age for all of his life, he said he would want to be ten years old.

> It is easy to see how badly my thoughts were confused. I vacillated constantly between feeling good and feeling bad, enjoying my actions and loathing myself, expressing remorse and seeking immediate pleasures. When I had changed my name, I had also vowed to change my bad habits and stop my illicit sexual activities. The vow was an empty gesture.

Art was constantly looking for new boys. One day he saw a ten-year old boy named Paul in a laundromat with

## The Case of Arthur Gary Bishop

his mother. He struck up a conversation with the boy and then with his mother. He told them he had a son about Paul's age and that it would be good for the two boys to get to know each other. He found that Paul only lived a short distance from him. Over a period of a few months he was able to gain the trust of Paul and his mother. Paul began coming over to Art's place and he and Jess became friends. He would come when Jess was there, and then later when Jess wasn't there. At first he would sleep on the couch, but later he would sleep with Art in his bed. Art coaxed Paul into letting him take pictures of his genitals using his "being blackmailed" scheme.

The blackmail scheme was the routine story that Art would tell to a boy in order to get his cooperation to take his picture. He would tell the boy that he was being blackmailed and that he didn't have the money to pay off the person blackmailing him. Art told Paul that the blackmailer had a sexual problem and wanted pictures of nude young boys as payment. Art told the boy that he would take a picture of his genitals and not his face and he would pay the boy $50.00 to let him do it. He could generally get the boy to agree since there would be no way to recognize who the boy was in the picture. (At times, however, he would take pictures of the boy's face as well without the boy's knowledge). When the police searched his place they found over 400 pictures of naked boys.

About this time, Art also met Tommy, age 8, and one night when Tommy came over for a slumber party with Jess and Paul, Art got him drunk and then took pictures of him. To pay the boys for these pictures, Art embezzled somewhere between $25,000 and $35,000 from his company. He started drinking but decided he didn't want to become addicted so he stopped. He became increasingly angry and his guilt plagued him because he couldn't stop his sexual cravings. Periodically he would remember some of his mission experiences but he would quickly put them out of his mind because they made him feel too much guilt. He got some puppies to appease his loneliness but that became an additional problem for him. The longest any of them lived before he killed them was three months.

> Many of them lasted only a few days or hours before I killed them. When the puppies piddled on the floor, or whined incessantly at night, it triggered my anger and I would mechanically proceed to drown, hit, or stab them to death. Many of the deaths were unnecessary and cruel and sadistic; my unconscionable cruelty seemed necessary if I were to appease that nagging craving in me that I can't define. Unfortunately, instead of satiating this urge, the dogs' deaths only increased my feeling of being unfulfilled… I knew it was wrong to take out my frustration on these helpless, defenseless animals but I felt as if I had little choice in the matter. As ironic as it sounds, I loved those puppies even if I was filled with a murderous hatred towards them.
>
> Many of the things I did were really sick and disgusting but, when push comes to shove, such

activities brought me too much immediate gratification for me to forsake them for long. I guess I adopted as my motto, "Do what you want, and damn the consequences."

There is a parallel between killing the dogs and the kids he murdered. As with boys, he loved the puppies, but little cute puppies grow up to be large adult dogs. His "murderous hatred" was partly towards the dogs, partly towards children, and partly towards himself. He was caught in a vicious sexual trap that he couldn't get out of and killing the puppies was not only a way to vent his anger, it was symbolic of the addiction that he couldn't change.

# Chapter 7

### October 20, 1981
### The Homicide of Danny Davis

One day when Art returned from work, he was lonely and wanted to find a boy who would engage in sexual activity with him. He wanted more than his pornographic pictures so he decided to find Paul and a friend of his named Tom for some sexual involvement. He drove past their house several times but couldn't see them so he gave up on them and began cruising, hoping he could locate a victim he could exploit. He drove around for a while but couldn't find a promising opportunity. Frustrated and lonely, he decided to return home. First, however, he would stop at a grocery store and pick up a few snacks.

Once he entered the store he saw a 4 year old boy named Danny Davis playing with some small toys in the toy aisle. Art's attention was immediately drawn to the boy. A man and woman were close to him so Art assumed they were his parents. However, they walked off and the boy was alone. Art sat next to the boy and pretended to look at some of the toys. He attempted to start up a conversation but the boy ignored him. Art told the boy that if he would follow him, there were some toys he could play with that he could keep. The boy still ignored him. Art leaned down and whispered strongly for the boy to come with him and then he turned and started walking away. The boy got up and followed him. Art kept a distance between himself and the boy in case someone noticed and questioned him about it. The boy followed him out of the store and when they reached a dark area of the parking lot, Art picked up the boy and carried him out of the parking lot toward his house, which was less than a block from the store.

The boy was too young for what Art was looking for and he considered sending the boy back to the store. But he couldn't pass up an opportunity. Art took him around the back of the store, through a field, and into the back of his house. He let the boy play with some toys while he got ready to kill the boy. As with Alonzo and to some degree with Kim, he felt a sense of detachment, as if "I'm not really doing this."

While he was killing the boy, the phone rang. It was Paul asking if he and Tom could come over and watch a movie. He told them they could. He hung up and hid the child's body. When the boys arrived they first wanted to go to the store and get something to have to eat while watching the movie.

When they entered the store Art could see a police officer talking to a store employee. Art approached the employee after the officer stepped away and asked if there was something wrong. She told him a man had misplaced his grandson. When Art saw the grandfather standing there he felt a sickening feeling. But then "I forced all feeling from my mind, and quickly left the store before I could see more."

Jess and Paul went home after the movie ended. Art then put the boy's body in a box and took him out to the trunk of his car.

The next day he drove to the Cedar Fort area where he had buried the other two bodies. After he had buried the boy, he noticed a truck parked on the road not far from where he was and was aware that the men in the truck could have seen him. He walked up and talked to them and found out that they were hunting deer and hadn't been aware of him. He told them he came out there to bury his favorite dog. They expressed their regrets and Art left. He thought, "Damn! I can be clever when I have to be."

This elation didn't last long. There was heavy media coverage regarding the missing boy, and each time Art saw the boy's smiling picture on TV, he felt nauseated.

> The missing posters for Danny at the local stores and restaurants haunted me whenever I saw them. I wished it would all be over and I could melt into oblivion. There was a large black van in a parking lot across the street from the grocery store

and Paul told me it was the search headquarters for Danny. Several times after work I walked by it and studied it. It fascinated and mesmerized me, as if it were temping and inviting me to come to it and confess. It would be better that way. I thought that I would be caught for sure. I was hoping to be caught. . . but nothing. No one approached me or questioned me further. I didn't have the guts to turn myself in.

He swore to himself that this was the last time he would kill. However, he was beginning to enjoy it.

*Art, you killed Alonzo to keep from getting caught by the police. Why did you continue killing after that?*

First, I had already broken a tremendously significant taboo by killing Alonzo. My feelings and emotions after his death were ambivalent. At times I felt empty and dammed by what I had done, but at other times I was disappointed in his death because the events associated with it were fading from my memory and becoming unreal. I didn't get any pleasure from the act of killing Alonzo, but I did derive sexual satisfaction before and after his death. As my recollection of his death grew dimmer, so did my sexual pleasure from the memory. I felt sad because it seemed somehow to make Alonzo's death less meaningful and significant. And that made his death unacceptable to me. It was as if I agreed with another part of my mind which insisted that "next time things will be done to make the murder more memorable." Therefore, murder was maintained as an acceptable act, at least in my mind.

Second, because I had killed before it was much easier to kill again. Much of the stigma and revulsion attached to murder were now gone, and a subconscious sense of "you can only go to Hell once" again made the thought of additional murder acceptable to me, especially when I considered only the possible pleasure promised by the sexual activity.

Art moved in with Jess and his mother to help save on expenses. While living there, there were times when he considered homicide but the opportunity wasn't available. Jess got a paper route and Art drove him around to deliver the papers. If Jess couldn't go, Art would deliver the papers for him. One day Art was delivering the papers and he had three left to go. He saw a boy about seven years of age. Art struck up a conversation with him and asked the boy if he wanted to help him deliver the next paper. The boy seemed excited about doing it so Art let him put the paper on the next porch, and then he let him do the next house as well. The final paper was going to be at a house about a block away. Art was impressed by the innocence and trust the boy had. He got very aroused by this and offered to let the boy deliver the final paper over on the next block. Fortunately the boy wouldn't go with him. Art said, "If that kid had gone with me, I would have kidnapped him and killed him. It seems that once that reflex is triggered, once the kid gets under my control, from that point on there's not much I can do but follow through almost automatically on whatever I'm going to do." Even though the boy wouldn't go with him voluntarily, he considered taking the boy by force. However, he didn't have a place to take the boy since, at that time, he was living with Jess and his mother.

Art said, "I had some vivid fantasies of the sexual pleasure I would have tried to get from him."

He began strongly resenting Jess and his mother and he decided that he needed a place of his own. He had moved back in with Jess and his mother in October, 1982. He moved out and got a place with a friend named Jordon in May, 1983. This gave him the freedom to do whatever he wanted without Jess or his mother detecting it. However, if he was going to bring a boy to his house he would have to plan around the times Jordan was there.

His sexual urges grew stronger and his desire to control them grew weaker. It would be only four months before he would be arrested for killing Graeme Cunningham.

# Chapter 8

### June 22, 1983
### The Homicide of Troy Ward

Art began growing marijuana in a section of his basement that he called the Grow Room. He wanted to keep it a secret but Jordan began telling his friends that created issues between Art and Jordan. He asked Jordan to move out.

One day Art went uptown to get some spring water for his marijuana plants and he saw a young boy, about 6 years old, standing on the corner. This was an opportunity he couldn't pass up. He stopped and asked the boy if he knew where he could find some spring water. The boy, Troy Ward, asked if he was looking for Liberty Park. Art asked Troy to go with him to show him where the park was. He took the boy to his house saying he would give him some ice cream. Art took him down in the basement, and in the guise of a game, handcuffed the boy's hands to a post and tied his legs to another post. He was molesting the boy when Jess called saying he needed a ride home. Art couldn't let Jess find Troy tied up like that, so he killed the boy. He went and picked up Jess and took him home and then returned to take Troy's body up Big Cottonwood Canyon and put it in the creek. Then,

> I returned home, but I was nervous. I couldn't go to sleep without a light on and I didn't dare go into the basement after dark. Jordan kept returning to the house to stay a couple of days. He was annoying me intensely but I couldn't say no to him. I was so upset I destroyed all the marijuana plants in my Grow Room. I was constantly on edge and getting upset about the slightest annoyances. I began to walk the streets of the neighborhood, hoping that the exercise would help, but it didn't. On two different occasions I tried to lure a young boy passing by into the house on the pretense of needing some help, but luckily for them, I didn't succeed.

This was very risky behavior. Art was constantly looking for boys to molest and he was taking greater chances, which would increase the probability of getting caught. If he had succeeded in getting a boy into his house, he would have killed him. Art was deteriorating rapidly now.

# Chapter 9

**Summer, 1983**
**Matt**

Jess had a friend named Matt. Art was attracted to the boy and he began planning to molest him and kill him. He would get the boy to come to his house under the guise of giving him the chance to earn some money. He was able to get Matt to his place and then downstairs where Art had a revolver (the one he killed Kim with).

> I think here is where I was beginning to get into feelings of what they call this abduction bonding that they talk about where you actually want to keep the boy with you, and maybe eventually I would have gotten to where I would have built a cage down in the basement, or maybe something

to keep a boy in. My plan was to get him down in the basement, pull the gun out on him, and say lie down here, and I'd tell him to handcuff himself to a post above his head. Just nice, quick, fast, slick. That's how it should have happened, but I got down there and I found myself stalling and pausing and like this isn't right. There is something wrong here. I don't know what it was, but I was very reluctant to follow through with it.

Matt seemed quite poised even though he was frightened. I felt some confusion. A lot of times as I carried out these murders I would just fall into a mechanical like reflex action, like you planned to do this now do it. But this wasn't happening here. I sat down and I put the gun down and I said Matt I'm sorry, I don't want to hurt you. Matt showed a lot of relief. I apologized to Matt again and I think I even had tears in my eyes. I went up to him and kind of embraced him. I didn't know the kid that well, but I just felt so bad about what I'd done. I really felt sorry at the time, kind of disgusted with myself. I pulled the gun out to show Matt the chamber in the gun was empty.

Art offered him money but Matt wouldn't take it. Matt wouldn't come over to Art's place again even if Jess was there. Marty would have undoubtedly reported him, but there were likely issues he had to resolve in his mind first, such as Art being Jess's friend. Would Art come after him and kill if he reported him? Would anyone believe Matt?

*What do you think happened to make you let him go?*

I don't know. Maybe it was because he told his sister that he was going with me. But that's not all of it. With some of the other boys I had a feeling that the boy was mine now and I can do whatever I want with him. With Matt this feeling wasn't there. It was more of a question of whether or not I really wanted to do it.

With the other boys before him, it seemed that some sort of a psychological thing would happen, but it just wasn't happening this time. With Matt it got to the point of it's now or never. I thought just pull out the gun and carry this out or forget about it. But I also thought just go back upstairs and take Matt to the skateboard park with Jess or whatever. But do something!

I remember I pulled the gun out and I felt very stupid doing it and to me it seemed I was very careful to not point it at Matt. I kind of pointed it off to the side. I didn't want to accidently shoot him. I'd left a bullet out of the firing chamber, but all I would have had to do was pull the trigger back and there would have been one in it. But I told Matt to lie down and he just kind of blanched. Like he was thinking I don't believe this. He sat down and motioned with his hands, take it easy. I think I ordered him to lie down and just let me handcuff him to the poles. I could tell he was troubled by this but he said, "No I'm not going to let you tie me up." He said, "Just put the gun away and let's talk." To me he seemed very cool. I could tell he was scared and everything.

*Okay, go on…*

In the first and second murders there was a feeling of detachment to some extent. This didn't happen with Matt. I was so completely aware of every single detail, like *Hey I'm doing this. This isn't some other guy, this is me.* Kind of like that feeling. I couldn't even aim the gun directly at Matt to threaten him to sit down. All of a sudden I felt a lot of revulsion of myself. I guess it was because I was aware of what was going on and finally I felt totally disarmed by Matt.

In the first three murders there was kind of an insulating numbness from it and I was kind of waiting for it to happen this time. I don't know how to explain this but you kind of wait for that to happen to engage. With Troy it didn't happen. With Matt it didn't happen. That's what saved him, and with Graeme it still didn't happen. I was very conscious of reality and I… I… I didn't want to be aware of it. I wanted to be out of the picture but at this point I knew, *Well, you're going to be in here.* At this point too I wondered should I stop this murder if I can or do I really want to? There was a lot of confusion here.

# Chapter 10

## The Last Two Months

Art had now deteriorated to the point of thinking about having a death chamber in his basement. It was becoming an all or nothing point for him, either continue to kill victims or stop all together. The conflict between these two choices was making him desperate and he was hoping that by escalating his violence he would find the excitement he was looking for. He would bring his victims into his basement, entice them into playing a game in which they would be handcuffed to a pole, sexually molest them, and then kill them. He did this with Troy Ward and he tried it with Matt. However, he wasn't getting any satisfaction from it. Matt was able to talk him out of it and once he let Matt go he was in extreme danger of being reported. If the police searched his home they would find hundreds of nude pictures of boys and they would find the room downstairs where he had held his victims captive. He managed his guilt by considering additional plans for kidnapping. The conflict between his guilt and his need for sexual activities was tearing him apart, but he couldn't stop what he was doing. He felt it was all right to take the chance because if he got caught he would commit suicide rather than being locked up again. It was either sex or suicide.

What was happening to him? He said, "Once I started doing things wrong in the beginning I wanted to go all the way with it."

Was it the conflict between his current psychopathic process and his earlier religious beliefs? Was it the break with his family? Was it that he believed that sooner or later the police would catch up to him and he would be arrested for his homicides, so he might as well get the most out of his victims before the police found him, and then commit suicide? Or was it what he feared the most, that people would find out about him and they wouldn't like him any longer.

It was likely a combination of all of these. He was more out of control than he wanted to be and it would soon culminate in a total collapse of his ability to control his emotions and his behavior. Art said the last two months were filled with confusion and uncertainty regarding what was happening within him. He felt he had become so evil that God wouldn't want him so it didn't matter what he did.

Without the boys in his life he had nothing. He needed them to salve his loneliness. He wanted to say to them,

"Hey, I want you to enjoy this, to savor this experience with me because this means a lot to me. This is my whole life. The most important thing in my life is the sexual things with you guys, and I want you to enjoy them too."

Art had stopped developing emotionally at about the age of ten and he would never mature beyond this age. He has=d become painfully aware that all youth would grow out of their childhood as Eric was doing. He would become powerfully attached to these boys and then they will be gone, leaving him even alone and lonely. Each loss of a companion was devastating and it wouldn't get any better. Each homicide was devastating too.

He was caught in a vicious killing cycle that he couldn't stop. He had partially dissociated during the first homicide and during the second. He was more fully aware of what he was doing during the third homicide and he didn't like it because he could see how evil he had become. The fourth and fifth homicides would give him no satisfaction at all. He was grasping at anything he could think of to bring him some happiness, but it wasn't working. Soon, however, it would all be over.

> I think I knew I would murder again if given the chance. In fact, I began to crave it. To me at that time there was no right or wrong in killing. I felt I had to do it. There was something [missing] in me that I had to fill. I don't know what it was, but it was there and I couldn't resist it.

What was it that created such an overwhelming craving in Arthur Bishop to kill a child? Ted Bundy's victims were adult women but it was the same craving force that Bishop had. Bundy called it an Entity and there were times he would verbally argue with this "thing" in him, trying to get it to leave him alone. He couldn't stop it.

Some people believe that it is the Devil or an evil spirit that is controlling them. Billy killed two teenage girls, was convicted of a double homicide, and was sentenced to life in prison. He gradually changed over the years and became religious. Billy talked about his experience of evil when committing his crime,

> I never *saw* any "demon" or "devil: during the commission of my crime. But, even while deriving the most twisted sense of glee and elation over the suffering of my victims, there were times when I experienced a sudden and intense feeling of being watched by a dark and evil presence. My skin would begin to crawl. My insides would begin to churn with a primal sense of terror. And I would turn my head suddenly, *expecting* to see something standing there behind me and yet understanding intuitively that this "something," if I saw it, would not be human. For years, I tried to explain that away as a figment of my imagination. But, as my walk with God over the years has worked a change in my nature, I've come to believe that evil is a real and living force—and was the very thing that made itself felt to me all those years ago.

*Art said,*

> I had these urges in me and they seemed to be gnawing away at me, always demanding to be released. I was always on the lookout for boys. At one time one killing would satiate a demand in me and after a homicide I lost the desire to do it again. But after Troy Ward, this didn't happen. I don't know how to describe it. It's just something I had to do. I didn't have any concern about the kids or their parents or society or my own family. I just felt I must do it.

# Chapter 11

### July 14, 1983
### The Homicide of Graeme Cunningham

I told Jess about this incident with Matt and at first he seemed to accept my apology. Later he called and said he had something for me. I went over and he gave me a note. It stated that he didn't want to see me anymore, that he had been trying to tell me for a year that he didn't want to see me anymore, even if I did give him gifts. I talked with him later and he finally agreed to keep visiting me if I would straighten up. We were back together but I knew we would discontinue seeing each other before too long. It was really depressing me. Jess was still dear to me and I had lost his friendship.

*It was about this time that you went on a trip to California, right? What was the purpose of the trip?*

>I planned a trip to California in the hopes it would ease some of the tension. Jess asked if he could invite a friend of his along. This friend was Graeme Cunningham. He had gone on camping and skiing trips with us before, and on several occasions had stayed overnight with Jess at my place. I had tried a few times to feel out Graeme while he was sleeping, and one time succeeded in feeling his bare genitals for just a moment, but he woke up and rolled over. From then on he always slept with his Levi's on when he came over.

*Why do you think Jess wanted Graeme to come along?*

>It was probably because he didn't want to be alone with me. If Graeme came with us then Jess and Graeme could do things together. Jess and Graeme were about the same age.

*What happened with Graeme? Why did you make the decision to kill him?*

>I was very attracted to Graeme. I called Graeme [the] Thursday night before we were to go to California about the things he would need for the trip. Then I asked him if he would like to make some money for the trip. He said yes, and agreed to meet me a short distance from his home. We went to my house and I acted like I was trying to make a phone call. [Art told Graeme that he wanted him

## The Case of Arthur Gary Bishop

to deliver a package to a person and he was supposedly trying to get in touch with the guy. It was a guise.] After 20 minutes [I told him] I was unable to complete it. I told him that I guess the deal was off, but I knew of another way he could make even more money.

Art told Graeme the story about being blackmailed. He said he owned a guy money but he didn't have the money to give to him. Art said the guy would reduce the debt if Art would provide him with pictures of boys' genitals. Art told Graeme that he would give him money for their trip to California if Graeme would allow him to take pictures of him.

> He was really reluctant to pose, but when I told him I would give him $150 he agreed. so I took the pictures. He was so nervous he wouldn't even try to get an erection and I was nervous because I didn't know what he was going to tell his parents about the $150. We finished the [picture taking] session and he started getting dressed.

At this point Art picked up a hammer and killed him.

> I was disgusted with myself. I liked Graeme but I had to kill him to satisfy my lusts. With Graeme I had a need to dominate him. To exploit him. To

possess him. That seemed to be the most important thing and somehow by killing him you do that. Somehow by killing him it seems like he becomes a part of you, or something similar to that. The boy is gone but because you were the one that did it somehow you're spiritually responsible for him. All of these thoughts happened within a matter of a few seconds. Graeme was sitting there on the bed getting dressed and at first it was like I wasn't in the room. I was aware of him there yet I wasn't aware of him there. But then something brought me back to reality. I loved him at this point. I thought, 'You've suffered enough. I'm not going to let anybody else hurt you. You're mine." Of all the murders, this was the hardest. I began to throw up.

Art went over to Jess's home to give him some money for the trip, but mostly to set-up an alibi. They would see that Art was alone so he wouldn't be connected to Graeme's disappearance.

>Stay. I don't want you to go yet. I knew I would never see him again. I knew I wanted him more than anything, but more than that I knew I was going to miss Graeme as a person. I felt an enormous loss for what I had done. I didn't want him to die. At this point I snapped out of it and said, "I'm not going to let myself feel sorry here."
>Graeme's death wasn't necessary. It was wrong to do it. I actually felt very alone without Graeme.

I thought, "How am I going to tell Jess? Or should I tell him?"

I was just too tired and didn't want to think about it. I felt that Jess was going to call me tomorrow and tell me about this and what was I going to say? It was like my mind said, "You are not going to worry about this now, it's not important." With Alonzo's death I felt that something had been ripped out of me. With Graeme's death I felt even emptier. I went back up to my bedroom and I brooded. I was really too tired to sleep. I was almost afraid to sleep. I said, "I'm not going to do this anymore. I've got to stop this. This is not worth it." It was reassuring to know that my pistol was there and all it would take was one motion in taking it out and firing it into myself. Yet, I thought, "You don't have the guts to do it. If you did you would have done it by now."

He then took Graeme's body up to the canyon and put it in the creek as he had done with Troy's body. When he was at the creek he thought:

I took Graeme's body up the canyon and put it in the creek like I had done with Troy's body. I survived the grief feelings for Graeme. It seemed that whenever the grief feelings would come strong, or would start to, the way I would overcome them would be to turn him into a sexual object.

# Chapter 12

## The Final Fling

Art, Jess, and Graeme were scheduled to leave for California early Saturday morning where they would take in Disneyland, Knott's Berry Farm, and other popular vacation sites. But now everything had changed. He knew that Mrs. Cunningham and Jess would be upset by Graeme's disappearance and of course that concerned him. However, as was his usual practice, he put it out of his mind. It's very difficult to understand how a person can take a life of another person and then pretend it hadn't happened. Through practice, Art had somehow learned to do it.

Art killed Graeme on Thursday night. This was his fifth victim. On Friday morning Jess called Art on the phone. He had wanted to get together with Graeme to work out last minutes details for the trip but Mrs. Cunningham told Jess that Graeme had left home and hadn't returned. Art pretended it was a surprise to him.

Art said to Jess, "That was stupid for Graeme to take off just before out trip. His mom probably won't let him go now."

Jess, who had been friends with Graeme for some time said, "I don't think he would have run off. I think something must have happened to him." He may have suspected that Art was involved in some way with Graeme's disappearance but he didn't raise his suspicions to Art until several days later. Jess wasn't sure that he wanted to go to California without Graeme but Art said they should keep to their plans. He said that Graeme would likely come back home in time for them leave on Saturday.

Jess kept in touch with Mrs. Cunningham on Friday to see if Graeme had returned. She said she and Graeme had had a little tiff the night before when Graeme got a phone call. His mother had asked him where he was going and he said he was going see a friend. She said she didn't believe him and he said he was going to a store and he left without any further explanation. She assumed that Graeme might have run away.

Art spent part of Friday night with Jess. He wanted to occupy Jess's time and not allow him to sit at home and worry about Graeme. Art sensed that this would be the last vacation he would take and he didn't want anything to mess it up.

☙

Saturday morning. Mrs. Cunningham said Graeme had still not returned. Art wanted to get on the road so they could get to Anaheim before it got too late but Jess was dragging his feet. He didn't want to go without Graeme and he would likely not have consented to the trip had not Art said that Graeme could come along as well. Jess was still mistrusting of Art after what had happened to his friend Matt.

Art continued to urge Jess to get started on their trip. Jess told Mrs. Cunningham that he would forgo the trip to see if he could help find Graeme but Mrs. Cunningham told them to go without him. There was no use giving up their vacation. Graeme would likely return home. Graeme had once asked Jess to run away with him and Jess later commented to Art that Graeme might have gotten angry over something at home and had run away without him.

It was about 10:00 a.m. when they started on their trip. Unlike the vacations Art and Jess had been on before, this one was stressful and empty of any real enjoyment. Jess was concerned about Graeme and periodically told Art that he wanted to call Jess's mother to see if Graeme had returned. Art was able to stall the phone calls. Art didn't want to receive bad news from home. It would ruin the trip. However, the trip was ruined from the moment he killed Graeme.

Art said, "I sensed that everything was going to come to a head quick."

He took Jess to a favorite BBQ restaurant while they were in California but Art became anxious when the thought came to him, "This is the last time you will be able to eat here." When they were at Knott's Berry Farm, Jess turned to Art and said, "It would have been so much more fun if I could have shown this to Graeme." Art cringed when Jess said this and again the thought came that it was all coming to an end.

"Art," I asked, "how do you keep from feeling guilt when you commit these crimes?"

He said, "I bury those feelings. It's like I have to if I want to maintain any sanity."

However, his subconscious was torturing him and he couldn't stop it. One section of his mind was addicted to his criminal behavior but another part was fighting against it. The war between who he wanted to be and who he had become was raging within him. He couldn't stop the internal struggle. There were only two ways to stop it. He had to either get caught or commit suicide. His career as a killer *was* coming to an end one way or another. He was fearful of this but sensed that he would not be able to stop it from happening.

They spent one week in California and were scheduled to return on Monday. Saturday, night Jess called his mother. She said the police wanted to talk to the two of them as soon as they got back. Art suggested they cut their trip short and leave Sunday morning.

On the trip back, Jess approached Art about his suspicions. He said, "You know, I've been thinking. It seems funny that you lived next to Alonzo and he disappeared. Kim was supposed to meet you about his skates and he disappeared. And you knew Graeme pretty well. It seems rather coincidental that you knew each of those kids and they disappeared. What do you think?"

Art commented simply, "Yeah, it does seem coincidental." Jess quickly followed up with, "But I don't think you would hurt anybody."

Art commented to me, "Jess had seen me in some pretty violent moods. I had temper tantrums but other than kicking Jess in the butt on one occasion I had never hurt him."

They drove on in silence.

༺༻

I asked Art if he got depressed on that California trip. He said, "As to suicide thoughts, the obscure thought was always in my mind as a possible escape route to avoid trouble in prison because of my thefts and molestation. After each murder I felt an urge to do away with myself. I had previously contemplated suicide but I was more serious about actually doing it after Graeme Cunningham's death. The thought crossed my mind to have a head on collision on my way back from California just prior to my arrest, but I didn't want to kill Jess too. At the police station, prior to my confession, I wanted to be able to return home. There I would leave a note telling about the boys before shooting myself. During June and July of 1983, I always felt on the verge of total frustration and suicide."

☙

Late on Sunday afternoon they had come a little over 400 miles. They were less than 200 miles from Salt Lake City when Art complained of a headache. He wanted to stop for the night in Beaver, Utah. Jess agreed to his request. Art had a favorite restaurant he wanted to go to. However, it was Sunday and the restaurant was closed.

Art said, "I was disappointed because I wanted one good last meal." They found a place that was open, but his "last meal" was like the past week—empty.

Even though it was fairly obvious at this point what would be coming when he got home, Art said that on the surface it still wasn't obvious to him. However, at a deeper gut level, he knew it would soon be all over.

☙

Monday morning he and Jess drove the rest of the way to Salt Lake. They stopped at Jess's home and talked to Jess's mom. Jess called Mrs. Cunningham and she asked Jess and Art to come over. Art was getting nervous and he asked Jess's mom if she had some medication he could take to calm him down. He didn't know what she gave him, but he took two pills then and kept two more for later.

When he got to Mrs. Cunningham's home she was extremely distraught. She asked Jess and Art to sit at a table with her. She handed them a pad and a pencil and asked them to write down the last time either of them had seen Graeme. Jess said he had seen her son sometime during Thursday. Art said he had been the one who called Graeme around 8:00 p.m. Thursday night. He said Graeme came to his place and picked a medical form to have his mother sign giving him permission to take Graeme to the hospital if he should get injured in California.

Mrs. Cunningham said, "Then you were the last one to see my son."

Mrs. Cunningham burst into tears during this discussion and had to leave the room to compose herself. Art didn't know it, but when she went into the other room she called the police.

Art commented to me about going over to her place, "I think it was good that I did. I likely never would have confessed had I not gone over. It bothered me that she was so distressed over losing Graeme."

Art had not been able to feel empathy for his victims, but once he saw what Mrs. Cunningham was going through he felt sympathy for her.

The police arrived at the Cunningham home within 20 minutes. Two officers talked to Jess and Art for a few minutes and then asked them to come down to the station to make a statement. The police had Art drive his car to the station but Jess was asked to ride with one of the officers.

# Chapter 13

## The Confession

On the way down to the station Art took the other two tranquilizers. When he arrived at the station, they asked Art to park his car in one of the No Parking areas. When Art asked about this, the officer said it was all right. They would take care of it.

Two officers talked to him for a while and Art professed he knew nothing about Graeme's disappearance. One or two years before, Art had created an alibi for himself in case he needed one. He had gone to the state of Washington, visited a small town, and had obtained Washington identification. If the police were ever to ask him about his whereabouts during their investigation of a homicide, he could say he had lived in Washington when the homicide occurred and he could show them his Washington identification. However, when he told these police officers that he had lived in Washington they asked him where he had lived, he couldn't remember the name of the town.

They asked him where he had gone to high school and he reported West High.

The officer asked, "Would you be in the yearbook?"

"Sure," Art answered, knowing that if they checked they would learn it was a lie.

"What was the address of your home?"

"I'm not really sure. We moved around a lot."

They continued along these same lines and it was becoming more and more clear that he was not being truthful. This went on for about 45 minutes and then Detective Don Bell came into the room. He had been talking to Jess.

Art said, "He played totally dumb, as if he didn't know anything about me."

However, Bell was a seasoned detective and he was attempting to learn what he could from Art before revealing what he already knew about him. Bell then asked him why he had pulled a gun on Matt. He also informed Art that he was also aware that he had been going by the name of Roger Downs and that this was not his real name. He told Bishop he was aware that before he became Roger Downs he was Lynn Jones and before that he was Arthur Bishop and as Arthur Bishop he had been found guilty of embezzlement and had skipped out on probation.

Art had no response to this. He felt relief that Detective Bell knew so much about him. Relief because he knew his life was out of control. He had decided in California that "… this wasn't the type of life I wanted. Anything was better than this. Even death."

Art said he wanted to confess that he had killed not only Graeme, but four others, but he didn't know how to do it. The police suggested he should have an attorney present, but Art said he didn't want an attorney because he would be counseled not to say anything to the police.

Art thought, "If they arrest me now I'll never have the courage to tell them. If they don't let me tell them I won't be able to later, and then I never will."

He believed he had to confess now or he would lose the courage to do it later. However, he couldn't bring himself to start the confession. After stalling for a couple of hours, he said, "If the ultimate has happened to Graeme, how long would it take for them to give and execute the death sentence?"

He said he was told it could happen in two to three months.

> At this point I felt it was very important to get it out. I just had to find a way to do it. I wanted to get it over with but at the same time I wanted to explain it so they could tell me where I had gone wrong to cause it to happen. Detective Bell has a lot of notes from that day. I'm just going from memory.

He was allowed to call Jess's mother. He told her that she would likely not see him again and that she should get

Jess into therapy. Detective Bell told Art, "I've talked to a lot of kids in my life and Jess is one of the most screwed up kids I've ever seen."

※

Art told the detectives that they needed to accompany him to his apartment as he had some things there that would help them understand him. Art signed over his rights to allow them to search his place. When they got there he opened a locked metal case that had pictures of the nude boys he had molested. He showed them a briefcase with the same type of material. He was trying to hint about the things he had done but felt they weren't listening.

Art said to the police, "I want you to understand so you can explain it to me. You're not understanding either."

They returned to the police station. Art was exasperated that he been unable to get them to understand what he was trying to convey to them. When they entered the room he blurted out, "Graeme is mine. I killed him." He went on to tell them the names of the other four boys he had killed, and that night he took them to the locations where he had deposited the bodies.

On the first day that I visited Art in prison, he expressed his disappointment in the police. They had done an excellent job in getting him to confess, but he said he agreed to confess the crimes only if they would give him mental health counseling and help him understand why he had killed his victims.

# Chapter 14

### Prison and Execution

Once Art was on Death Row and had no opportunity to molest children, he began to return to his religious self again. As he got closer to his execution he began wearing his earphones when he listened to his radio and when he was reading. He didn't want to listen to the vulgar talk of some of the other inmates. He began reading his scriptures again and requested religious music. On the night of his execution I spent an hour with him and then his religious leader spent an hour, and we went back and forth like this. He had his scriptures with him.

He seemed relaxed and he said he was ready to die. He appeared to have a better understanding of how he had become a pedophile. He said he wasn't afraid to meet God, but he said the one thing he was fearful of was of meeting the kids he'd killed and having to explain to them why he'd killed them. He gave me a copy of his "last words" to take to the press and just before midnight he was strapped down on a gurney and a hood was put over his head. He was taken to the death chamber where he was executed shortly after midnight.

# Epilogue

When Art was on Death Row, he struggled with the perception of what and who he had become. Had he not seen what was happening to him somewhere along the line? I believe he had some brief recognition that something was wrong when he was 14 years old and saw that 7 year old boy swimming. When he was attracted to him and wanted to see his genitals, he figured that in order to sexually fondle him he would have to kill the boy first. That thought shocked him and frightened him initially. However, after that he entered the beginning stage of pedophilia and gave in to his impulses. He began to believe that he was different from the other boys his age. He kept it secret which minimized his chances of getting caught and he allowed himself to indulge in his fantasies. Without realizing it, he was creating a sexual addiction.

From this point, Art created two aspects to his personality. On one hand he had a dream of getting married, having a good job, and raising a family. On the other hand his primary interest was in children below the age of puberty. He developed a fantasy life consisting of him surrounded by children and he tried to shape his real life to fit this fantasy. Since he mostly fantasized about kids, that side of him became intense and complex while the "normal" side of him withered away. When he molested boys he felt bad about what he was doing, but this didn't stop him from doing it. His primary defense against depression and loneliness was to be with children. He played with them, helped them with their homework, bought them gifts, and took them on trips, such as skiing, camping, and even to Disneyland, which was nearly one thousand miles from his home in Salt Lake City. His world revolved around children and it became sexualized. He would turn to sexual fantasies to relieve his depression and loneliness but this in turn only increased them. It quickly became a vicious cycle and he lost control almost from the start.

He struggled with his dual nature. He wanted to stop hurting kids, but at the same time he didn't want to stop. He was enjoying molesting kids, but at the same time he was becoming more disgusted with himself for doing so. Finally, he got caught. To some it appeared that he had set himself up to get caught but, if so, he was unaware that he was doing it.

He was relieved to be in prison and on Death Row but at the same time he was unhappy that none of the things he'd dreamed for would occur. He would have no wife, no children, no job, and no kids as friends. Everyone hated him. All he could really look forward to was his death.

Art had vivid dreams in prison that reflected his internal struggles. Some the dreams he wrote about are quite revealing. This is one of them:

> *I had been given permission to go home for a special visit with my family—the only restriction was that I had to be handcuffed at all times. I discovered that the handcuffs were on so loosely that I could easily slip my hands out of them. I showed Mom that my hands were free and told her that now was my chance to escape. She surprised me when she agreed, and together we devised an escape plan. She had a friend who lived out of state who would let me live with him and his family. He had a young son, about 6, and Mom made me solemnly promise to her that I would not abuse nor hurt the boy in any way. I quickly agreed without a second thought, and she proceeded to make the necessary arrangements.*
>
> *I climbed into the back of the truck taking me to my destination and hid. It was going to be a long ride. As the truck sped down the highway, through a huge hole in the floorboards I could see the asphalt rushing by beneath the truck. I suddenly remembered with a*

*pang of hurt the promise I had made to Mom. I realized that I couldn't keep that promise, that in time my resolve would weaken and I would eventually have to molest the boy. I began crawling closer to the hole so I could fall to my death from the speeding truck.*

This dream says a lot about Art. Let's take a look at it:

*I had been given permission to go home for a special visit with my family*

Art wanted to see his family. There were a few visits and some cards and letters from his family when he was in prison, but not what he would have liked. The end would be coming and he would never have the chance to see them again. He was wishing for them to visit.

*I discovered that the handcuffs were on so loosely that I could easily slip my hands out of them.*

Art had narcissistic characteristics. He prided himself on the idea that he could lie to people in authority and get away with it. At times he felt quite superior. The loose handcuffs showed his disdain for the competence of people in charge. They couldn't even put handcuffs on right. He was able to *easily slip my hands out of them.*

*I showed Mom that my hands were free*

Art had a strong bond with his mother. He had a desire to please her over anyone else in his life. In the dream she agrees to help him escape. I met his mother. She would never agree to his escape. For Art, he couldn't simply do something on his own, including escape. He has to have approval and he usually wanted it from his mother.

> *She had a friend who lived out of state who would let me live with him and his family. He had a young son, about 6, and Mom made me solemnly promise to her that I would not abuse nor hurt the boy in any way. I quickly agreed without a second thought, and she proceeded to make the necessary arrangements.*

The primary point of the dream is that he wants to be with a child again. Everything prior to this in the dream provides a way for him to do so. His mother is trusting and, without yet realizing it, Art is deceiving. He will agree to anything at this point in order to be with a child again.

> *I suddenly remembered with a pang of hurt the promise I had made to Mom. I realized that I couldn't keep that promise, that in time my resolve would weaken and I would eventually have to molest the boy. I began crawling closer to the hole so I could fall to my death from the speeding truck.*

If he once again molested a boy it would severely hurt his mother and she would totally give up on him. He couldn't live with that. Also, molesting a child would put him back into the same situation he was in before he got caught. The concluding message is that the only way he can keep from causing more trouble is to be dead.

Art had other dreams that reflected his struggle with his impulses. It's unfortunate that he could not have been aware earlier in his life what his subconscious mind was trying to tell him through his dreams while he was on Death Row.

It's tragic that five innocent boys were forced to give up their lives in order to satisfy his psychopathic desires. Hopefully, we will find a way to recognize when a serious psychological problem is beginning to develop in an individual at a point when we can perhaps do something to keep it from becoming psychopathic.

# Part Two:
# The Case of Westley Allen Dodd

# Preface

There are very few people in the world as evil as was Westley Allan Dodd.

He murdered three children and was planning to take the lives of many more. Had he not been caught while attempting to kidnap a fourth child, he would likely have killed several more before he was finally apprehended.

No one who knew him when he was a child would have predicted that he would become a child serial killer; he seemed as normal as any other kid. Before the age of nine there were a few signs that he was starting to develop an interest in sexual exploration. He and a cousin and another boy touched their penises together while getting dressed after playing in a portable pool in his cousin's back yard. Two weeks later he pulled down his swimming trunks to his knees and waded around the pool in his own yard. Then he took off his swimming trunks and waded around the pool naked.

There is nothing evil about this behavior. It's not uncommon for children of that age to explore their own and each other's anatomy. However, with Wes it didn't stop there. He wasn't emotionally close with his family and had few real friends, and was experiencing emptiness in his life. The adrenalin rush from these activities had a strong effect on him. He continued with this sexual exploration and gradually became obsessed with wanting to do more and more.

Children didn't become his targets until he was around 13 years old. Wes exposed himself to a few children and he believed they liked it. This became a major turning point in his life and even though he got caught, he refused to quit doing it. He escalated in his sexual activity and by the age of 15 his primary goal in life was to molest children. By age 24 he was planning to kill a child, and at the age of 28 he carried out his plan. He kept a journal of his homicides. His objective was to continue kidnapping and killing more children.

My first introduction to Westley Allan Dodd came in August of 1992 when I happened to catch a small part of an interview the press had with him. By then, I had worked with sex offenders and killers in Utah State Prison for close to 20 years and I was quite familiar with their motivations and techniques.

## The Case of Westley Allan Dodd

I was intrigued by the fact that Dodd killed two boys on Labor Day of 1989 and shortly after that kidnapped and killed a third child. He was soon apprehended while attempting to kidnap a fourth child. It's relatively rare for child sex offenders to kill their victims and even more rare for a killer to take the lives of multiple children in such a short period of time.

I knew there was something different about *this* child killer. He had become a psychopath, but unlike most psychopaths he said he wanted to die for his crimes. He even went so far as to threaten that if society were to ever let him go (which of course would never happen) he would go on kidnapping children. Perhaps his desire to die was simply an easy way out of this life. After all, if he couldn't have children to molest, why stick around? However, when he was given a choice of *how* he wanted to be executed, he could have chosen lethal injection, a relatively humane way to die. He would have simply gone to sleep and it would have been all over. Instead he requested to die by hanging, saying he didn't deserve anything better than what he had done to one of his victims. Is this the typical voice of a psychopath?

It's generally believed that Wes was only interested in sex with male children, but this isn't true. Wes had a few female victims as well. And some reports indicate that his sexual interest was only in children. This isn't accurate, either. He had a girlfriend. For the few weeks they were together, they had sex three or four times a week. Wes said he enjoyed sex with her and he planned to continue with the relationship. He then threw his pornographic pictures of children in the trash when he and his girlfriend talked about getting married. He looked forward to settling down with a wife and family. But then something went wrong and he returned to his plan to kill children.

I was intrigued by his openness and I wanted to include him in my research on serial homicide. I submitted a request to Wes for an interview and he promptly granted my request. Mr. Jerry Davis, Administrative Assistant at the Washington State Penitentiary in Wala, Washington, approved the visits.

The first time I visited Wes on Death Row at the prison he was escorted into a small room separated into two sections with a thick Plexiglas partition. Each side of the partition had a stool and we talked loudly through a wire-covered opening. He was dressed in an orange jumpsuit.

As with Bishop, Dodd said he wanted to help put a stop to child molestation. Interestingly, just as with Bishop, Dodd said the second thing he wanted from my research on him was to understand how it all happened. He fully admitted to killing the three children and he said he was happy that he got caught because otherwise he would have continued molesting and killing more children. Bishop had said that same thing. Dodd said he just didn't understand how he got to be that way in the first place. Arthur Bishop felt the same.

I met with Wes on multiple occasions, and obtained several hours of recorded material. He began writing and sending his history to me in the beginning of September, 1992 and continued providing additional history through December, totaling over 200 pages.

At the bottom of one of his first letters, he wrote:

> I'll stop here and mail this much. You'll no doubt have questions. While I wait for them, I'll be writing from age 11 on. Write as often as you can/want. Time is critical. I've been on Death Row over 2 years now and I am not appealing my sentence, so time may be short. We should do all we can as fast as we can. I have two main motivations, well, three. 1) To learn why it all happened and how I could actually kill, 2) to help psychologists learn how to stop others before they kill, and 3) by co-operating and helping you stop others. . . to help protect other potential victims. Bye for now.

The last I saw him at the prison was a couple of weeks before his execution. He was executed by hanging at 12:05 a.m. on January 5, 1993.

# Chapter 1

## Washington State Penitentiary

September 1992.

*Wes, you're here on Death Row for killing children. You may be executed but you don't seem very worried about it, or is it just that you're trying to hide your fear? I think that most people would be terrified knowing that they will soon die, particularly for killing a child. Does this bother you very much?*

>No, not a lot. My attorney wants me to call it off but I don't want to. I had to petition the court to allow me to go ahead with the execution.

*But why are you in such a hurry to die?*

> I really don't have anything to live for. When I was sentenced for death, I told everyone that they had better watch me closely because if I had the opportunity to do so, I would kill anyone I could. If I were ever able to get out of prison, I would go on killing kids. I wanted them to be afraid of me so they would execute me.

*Do you really believe that you would kill other children if you were ever to get out of prison?*

> Yeah, I have no doubt about it. The obsession is too strong for me to be able to stop.

*Tell me, why did you select hanging? A lethal injection would be a much easier way to die than to go by hanging.*

[Wes took a deep breath, paused for several moments, and continued.]

> I killed Lee Islie early in the morning before I had to go to work. I hung his body in my closet because I was in a new apartment and I didn't want my landlady to come in to check out my place and find him dead. I don't feel that I deserve any better way to die than what I did to him.

*Wes, people see you as a coldblooded killer. You molested children for several years and then you finally turned to murder. But you don't have the appearance that most people think of as a killer. I can picture you more as a clerk in a store than as a killer of kids.*

Yeah, others have said the same thing. I did work in a few places and I enjoyed it.

*Did your bosses like your work?*

My bosses always complemented me. I got promoted to manager positions because I caught on fast as to what had to be done and I followed orders. My bosses trusted me.

*But what happened? If I hear you right, you were a store clerk...*

I managed a store, a couple of them in fact.

*Were you molesting children during the same period of time?*

I'd complete my shift and then I'd go home and fantasize about children I'd seen in the store during the day. I only lived a short distance from my work in this one job and I'd sometimes walk to work. It wasn't that I couldn't drive. I wanted to make friends with people in my neighborhood.

*What was the purpose of doing that?*

I wanted the people to know me. When they see a person living in their neighborhood who is friendly, and stops to talk to them, they develop a trust for him. I got to know the people and, in particular, the children. I planned ways to kidnap them and molest them.

*So having a good job where you were trusted and living in a neighborhood where people had also come to trust you didn't have any influence on whether or not you were going to continue molesting children?*

> The problem was that molesting children was all I wanted to do at that time. I don't know if it was that I couldn't stop or just didn't want to stop.

*What about family or friends? Is there anything they could have done to have kept you from killing those three children?*

> I didn't have any friends and my family didn't exist.

*What do you mean, didn't exist?*

> I have never been close to my family. My dad comes to see me now. This is the best relationship I have had with him for years but back then my parents didn't seem to care very much about me.

*Do you really believe that?*

> They say they did but I never believed it.

*Wes, how old were you when you first thought about killing a child?*

> Twenty-four.

*How old were you when you started molesting children?*

> I began exposing to them when I was about 13 years old.

*Was your sexual interest always towards boys?*

> When I first had an interest in molesting children, I didn't care if it was a boy or a girl.

*Did you ever have a sexual interest towards girls?*

> Yeah, but girls in junior high school made fun of me. I lost my virginity in a one night sexual encounter with a girl but Cassie is the only woman I've had a sexual interest in, but that's because she initiated the sex.

*You're talking about your girlfriend?*

> Yeah. I could have selected boys or girls as victims and there were times that I molested girls as well. I selected boys because they were less likely to report me.

*Did you ever have a desire to kill anybody when you were a child?*

> No, my childhood was pretty normal.

Up to now in the interview, we had touched on several topics and I felt he was open to talk about any of them. He was known for sexually molesting boys but he said at first he didn't have a strong preference for boys or girls. Why girls? And, if he had a sexual interest in a girlfriend named Cassie, and should that relationship have worked out, would he have stopped molesting children? If his objective was to molest children, why did he feel he had to kill a child?

I had many questions that I wanted to continue asking but I decided at this point to explore his early history to determine how it all might have begun and to go from there. However, I had one more pressing question before getting into his childhood.

# Chapter 2

### Contract with Satan

*All right, I'd like to start at the beginning and find out when and how the sexual problem first began and why it reached the point that you felt you had to kill a child. But before we get to your history, talk about what led up to your decision to kill your first two victims, the Neer brothers.*

[Wes stood up and walked around the room as if he was trying to collect his thoughts. I wasn't sure whether he wanted to talk about killing the Neer boys or not, but then he returned to his seat and began his story.]

In October of 1989—I was 28 years old at the time—my girlfriend Cassie left me and she took my son with her.

*You had a son?*

Yeah, his name is Bobby. Cassie was his mother. I didn't know at first that Bobby was my son. I had been living with a friend named Ralph, and Cassie, her mother, and her two children were staying with us. We were living in Buckley [Washington]. Cassie wanted to move to Yakima, closer to all her friends, and Cassie talked me into moving to Yakima with her. I quit my job and went, leaving most of my stuff behind. I wanted to start all over with Cassie. We left when Ralph was at work without telling him we were leaving. As I loaded up the U-Haul, Cassie told me she had something she needed to tell me. She hadn't told me before because she thought I'd be mad.

She told me that Bobby was my son. When I thought back, I could see that Bobby was born nine months after that first night that Cassie and I had sex [in May, 1989]. I wasn't mad. I was very happy. I was a father. I had a son!

With no job and no place to live, no job prospects, and no one I knew in Yakima, and with $300 in my picket, I rented a U-Haul trailer and moved myself, Cassie, her two children, and her mother to a motel in Yakima.

I threw away all of my pornography of kids that I had been collecting because I thought I would get a job and we would be a family. The motel cost $200 for that first week and towards the end of the week I ran out of money and Cassie's welfare check hadn't come yet. One evening Cassie and her mother got dressed and said they were going out and they left me to take care of Bobby and Cassie's son, Robert.

*Where were they going?*

Cassie had told me that she was into witchcraft, as was her mother, and I suspected that both of them were prostitutes.

*Were you all right with that?*

That was okay with me because we needed the money.

*Did they come back?*

They didn't come back that night.

*How did you feel about that?*

It bothered me but I assumed they would be back in the morning. In the morning her old boyfriend came and took my son [and Robert] and their clothes and when he left he told me I would never see Cassie or my child again.

*Wow, that must have really hurt.*

I was devastated. I had no job and I had run out of money. I had a strong urge to kill myself. I didn't know what to do. I didn't care if Cassie and I stayed together but it really hurt to lose my son.

*Enough to consider suicide?*

> Yes. I had quit my job for her and her mother. I knew I could get another job but Bobby was *my* child. I would finally have a child that I could raise. I was a father! I couldn't give him up.

*Did you try to argue with the guy who came for her belongings?*

> No, I just let him take them. I knew he wouldn't tell me where they were.

*What did you do?*

> I called my father in Vancouver and he said I could come back and stay with him and my stepmother until I got on my feet again. The problem was that I didn't have any money for gas, but I remembered I had some tools in my car. I sold them for $10.00, enough to buy gas to get me to my dad's place.

*So you were depressed and angry, but how did that make you want to kill a child?*

> On the way up to Vancouver I decided that I would molest children again and this time I would make sure that they wouldn't leave me.

*What do you mean?*

> I would kidnap them and keep them as sex slaves.

Wes went on to talk about a previous attempt to call on Satan to help him get children, but it didn't work. He had tried to kidnap a child to kill on a previous occasion but something came up to stop it. He decided to try again but this time he would kill a child as an experiment to see if he could actually do it.

> As I left Yakima I knew I would kill. No half-hearted attempts or plans like before. I was going to kill, and while not really believing in all that Satan stuff, I was going to ask Satan to help me. It was on that drive that I decided to write a contract with Satan. My soul for kids to rape and kill.

On his way back to Vancouver, Wes picked up a hitchhiker who began talking to him about child pornography. Wes dropped him off at a junction that had a small convenience store and a couple of other buildings, a seemingly strange place to drop off a hitchhiker.

Wes dismissed it at first but a couple of days later he began thinking of it again. Wes had said nothing of child molestation or of pornography to the hitchhiker before he brought it up. If this conversation had not originated with the Devil, he reasoned, why did child pornography even come up? After all, hitchhikers don't usually get in your car and begin talking about it. At first he was puzzled and he didn't ascribe it as an answer from Satan. But that would soon change.

When he got back to Vancouver, Wes stayed with his father and stepmother. Wes's parents had planned a week-long vacation and they took him with them. It was during this vacation that Wes sought the help of the Devil to carry out his plan. As he rode in the back seat of his father's car on the way to their vacation destination he considered his options.

> On the following Sunday I wrote a three-page "legal" document promising my soul to Satan in return for the undetected opportunity to kill children. I promised Satan that I would have future victims sign their souls over to him.

*But Wes, if it didn't work the first time and if you didn't have more than a cursory belief in the Devil, why did you think it might work this time?*

> It must have been July 30th when I wrote the contract with Satan, a Sunday, the day you're supposed to worship God. I didn't expect it to really work, but if I was going to do it, and if Satan was real and would help, then God's holy day would be the day to ask.
>
> It was a three-page contract. I don't remember now what all I wrote, but Satan was to provide me with whatever I'd need to locate and kidnap kids without being seen. I could use the kids in any way I desired and they would sign their own lives over to Satan before dying.

Wes then played a game to ask Satan how many children the Devil would initially give him to kill. The answer came back: Three. With this and the experience with the hitchhiker, Wes was now fairly convinced that Satan was going to grant him his wishes.

As it turned out, Westley Dodd killed three children. He made an attempt to kidnap another child but failed. He then made one more attempt and failed again. That time his truck broke down a few blocks from where he had made his attempt and the police caught him.

※

The question has been raised whether I personally believe that Satan really honored the contract Wes made with him. Did Satan cause these three children to be killed by Wes? The first time he attempted to make a contract with Satan, he didn't have a strong belief in Satan, or in the likelihood the Devil would help him. However, the second time, Wes seemed to be sincere in seeking Satan's help.

In his first attempt to bargain with the Devil, he laid out a pentagram and some candles, but he felt a bit silly and put them away. The second time, however, he wanted to show Satan he was serious about wanting help. He wrote out a contact offering his soul and the souls of his victims to Satan. However, he didn't seem to remember that he had created the contract until after he was picked up by the police.

By his own statements, Wes did not dedicate the souls of the Neer boys to Satan, and when he kidnapped Lee Isley he didn't dedicate him or his death to Satan either. Regardless of my personal beliefs, Wes's own actions show that he didn't really believe anything would come of his gesture. If Wes didn't believe in Satan's help, there's no reason I can see that I should give more credence to that possibility than Wes did.

# Chapter 3

## Early Childhood

*Wes, before we get into how and why you killed the three children, I'd like to start at the beginning and talk about how you got to the point where you could take the life of an innocent child.*

> When I was young I had no thoughts of wanting to harm a child. If anybody had told me then that the day would come that I would not only want to molest children, I would want to kill them, I would have thought they were crazy.

*Then how did you get to that point in your life where you could actually carry it out? I mean, did you consider yourself to be crazy when you made the decision to commit murder?*

No, not really. It was just something I felt I had to do to keep from getting caught and put in jail again.

*But why torture a child?*

I don't know for sure. In some ways I wanted to be a scientist. I wanted to medically explore bodies and to keep notes on my findings.

*Wes, it's hard for me to understand how a person could be that cruel and then turn around and want me to write about it so that society could figure out ways to prevent it from happening to others in the future.*

*It's almost as if there are two sides to your personality, one side that gets off on molesting and torturing a child and another side that has some level of compassion and wants to protect children from people like you in the future. Or could it be that what appears to be compassion is only a desire for recognition and to make it appear that you care when, in fact, you really don't care?*

I really don't know, maybe a little of both.

*Wes, let's start at the beginning. Tell me about your parents. Where did they come from? What were they like?*

[He leaned forward so I could hear him.]

My mother's family came from Oklahoma and my father's side came from Montana. My father grew up on a dairy farm near Kirkland and he completed high school and two years at Yakima Valley College. My parents met in high school and got married in 1960. I was their first child. I was born in Kennewick, Washington on July 3, 1961.

We moved to Kirkland [Washington] where my brother George was born on June 5, 1962. Later we moved back to Kennewick, close to where Dad's parents lived, where my sister Kaylee was born on May 29, 1965. My father worked in a creamery with his grandfather.

*Well, that all sounds very normal. Were you unhappy?*

We had a large garden with a fishpond and it had a waterfall going into it. We had all the toys a child would want. We had racecar sets, electric trains, and the usual tricycles. We even had our own merry-go-round in our backyard.

*Wow. I didn't have half of those things. It sounds like you had an ideal childhood. Your parents must have cared for you very much.*

I was a quiet child. I didn't socialize with the other kids very well.

*Was there anything wrong to cause you to be like that?*

After I came to prison, my dad visited me. When we talked about all of this he said that when my brother was born I crawled into a corner and never came out.

*What do you think your father meant by that? Do you think you were jealous of your brother when he was born?*

> I was too young to remember that specific event but I do remember that I was always jealous of my brother and my sister. I always felt that Dad and Mom favored them. I remember when I had my tonsils out. Dad didn't come to visit me in the hospital but he did go to the hospital later when my brother and sister got theirs out.

*Did you feel that your parents loved your younger brother and sister more than they loved you?*

> Dad said I was the center of attention until they came along. After they were born I withdrew emotionally. For some reason I was always jealous of them.

Wes didn't show any serious behavior problems at the time, so his withdrawal was not taken to be a major concern.

However, Wes felt abandoned. He said he didn't bond with his parents in his early childhood. This problem began with the birth of his brother and was made more permanent when his sister was born. It was consistently reinforced throughout his life each time he felt his parents cared more for his brother and sister than for him.

The bonding of a child to his parents is the beginning of love. Wes said he didn't feel love from his parents when he was a small child. It likely was there but he was too sensitive about the attention he saw his parents giving to his siblings. When I talked to him in prison, he expressed confusion about what love was and he believed there never had been any love in his home. His brother refuted this. It appears that the love was there but Wes was unaware of it. If there was no perception of love, there likely would have been less of a capability to feel guilt.

Wes's happiness came from his toys and his playmates. However, without the requisite ability to feel guilt there was little to stop him from developing destructive thrills as well.

*Wes, were you sad or lonely when you were a child?*

> No, I had my toys and I was comfortable playing with them by myself. And there were always cousins around and I had a few friends in my neighborhood.

*Did things go all right at your cousin's place?*

> My cousin had a wading pool in his backyard and he and another cousin and I were getting dressed. My cousin and this other boy touched their sex organs together and my cousin asked if I wanted to do it. I did it with them.

*And?*

> It was fun. Me and my brother slept in the same bed together and we took our baths together until we were six or seven years old so nakedness was not foreign to me. However, there was some-

thing about doing this with my cousins that was different.

*What do you mean?*

It must have woke some part of me because I suddenly started doing other sexual things I'd never done before.

*Like what?*

I knew it was wrong and that's what made it exciting. Two weeks later while I was in the swimming pool in my own backyard I pulled my swimming trunks down my knees and swam around the pool.

*Do you have any memory of why you did that?*

I don't know why, I'd never done anything like it before, and I don't know if I'd even heard of such a thing being done by anyone else. I can only remember that it was exciting. My heart was pounding, and I just knew it was something I shouldn't do.

A short time after that I swiped my mother's lotion and I rubbed it on my stomach and groin. I don't remember getting sexually aroused, but there was a big adrenalin rush. I knew I would be embarrassed if my mother found out where I put her lotion, but she didn't find out.

*Did it seem wrong to do it?*

Yeah, I knew it was wrong but I didn't feel any guilt over it.

There was another thing that happened right after that. My brother and I wore pajamas but one night I went to bed nude. My brother reported it to my father and I got in trouble for it.

Dad yelled and told me to get dressed. I said, "Why? You sleep naked." He said he was hot. That made me angry. I was hot too. It was a hot summer night. Dad slept naked but I wasn't allowed to. I just didn't understand. I didn't dare argue, but I remember comparing that to Dad's own favorite saying, "Goddamn it quit your swearing."

*So did you stop doing those things?*

No. I enjoyed it. I began to feel that if it's wrong but fun, it's all the more exciting.

# Chapter 4

## Move to Umatilla

In the spring of 1971, Wes's father was transferred to Umatilla, Oregon. Wes enjoyed the move and the new house. There were the usual family camping and picnics almost every weekend and it was a happy time for him. He enjoyed living close to his father's relatives. However, in spite of these happy times, Wes's interest in sex was increasing.

During the summer following the $4^{th}$ grade, he and his sister were in a garage with a neighbor girl. The friend pulled down her pants to allow Wes and his sister to look at her, and Wes followed suit. His sister looked at his sexual parts but the neighbor girl wouldn't, telling him she had seen it before.

I remember feeling disappointed that D— wouldn't look at me.

*Did you get away with it?*

My brother learned about it and reported it to my mother. I denied it and Mom dismissed the incident by telling me it was nasty and to not do it again. I think she believed me and I didn't get into any big trouble over it.

*You got caught trying to sleep naked in your bed and now you were reported for doing this. Did it make you want to stop doing these things?*

No. I wasn't doing anything seriously wrong. It didn't feel wrong and, except for Dad yelling at me, I didn't get punished.

**Fifth and Sixth Grades**

In the spring of 1972 when Wes was in the 5th grade, his father was hospitalized with asthma and had to find a new job where there was less of a risk for another attack. The family moved to Richland to be near relatives, which pleased Wes. The new location, near parks, playgrounds, and two rivers, was an open opportunity for play and excitement. His father took a night job as a janitor and his mother obtained employment as a daytime cook.

Dad made me and Gary help him with his janitorial work. The heavier part of it fell on my shoulders because I was the oldest. I complained about it but I was made to feel like I was a bad boy if I didn't help out. But with less time to do homework my grades suffered. Dad yelled at me for that. I was getting more angry at my father.

*Wasn't your father a role model for you?*

No.

*Did you have any role models in your life?*

No. There wasn't anyone in my life that I wanted to pattern myself after. I had no close friends so I was spending a lot of time alone.

# Chapter 5

## The Smallest and Youngest

*Wes, what was junior high like for you?*

Since my birthday was on July the 3$^{rd}$, I was one of the youngest kids in my class. I felt inferior to the other boys in several ways. They were older and bigger. I was one of the slowest and weakest and most uncoordinated kids in my class and I was painfully aware of it.

After a gym class I had to shower with the other boys. I was immature and I didn't understand locker room jokes. On one occasion while I was waiting to take a shower in PE, another boy offered to share *his* with me. The other boys burst out laughing. I didn't know what he was referring to but I knew I was the object of the joke.

*Did that happen very often?*

Quite often. On one occasion a girl in my health class told me my epidermis was showing. I didn't know what she was referring to and I was embarrassed. I looked down to see if I was unzipped and she started laughing. She told her friends about it and they giggled when they passed me in the hall.

*What effect did that have on you?*

I stayed away from the other kids as much as I could. I became a loner. I felt bad because I wasn't part of my family and I didn't fit in with the other kids at school.

*Was academics an outlet for you?*

I had an unusual interest when I was in 7th grade history. I got D's in the class, but one particular topic fascinated me. The Nazi death camps.

We watched a filmstrip about them one day. It showed us pictures of nude men, women, and children lined up together waiting for their turn in the shower room. It showed the nude bodies of adults and kids being tossed into large pits or pushed into them with bulldozers. I remember going to the school library's visual room checking out all the film clips I could find about the Nazi death camps, looking for more of those pictures. I wished they'd had better cameras and colored film when the pictures were taken.

So, at age 12, I was fascinated by death and nudity. A few months later I'd forgotten all about it.

> I didn't remember this until I started searching for answers from my Death Row cell, trying to figure out how it all started.
>
> I've tried to figure out when it all started. Originally, I thought it began in the spring of 1975, at age 13, or maybe two or three months before my 14$^{th}$ birthday. But as I look back, occasionally recalling other events and thoughts from the past, it started much earlier.

Wes talked about a time when he was 12 years old. He was watching a program on TV and the studio operator accidently switched over to a pornographic film that he was watching. Wes saw it but wasn't clear about what he was seeing in the few seconds that it was on. He saw a person lying on their back getting their chest painted. Since the person's breasts were small, he thought it was a man. The next day Wes's friend was over at his house. Wes's father asked if either of them had seen it. Wes said he had but he thought it was a man since the person had small breasts.

> But right there in front of my only friend in the world, Dad took great pleasure in thoroughly humiliating me, teasing me about not knowing the difference between men and women. If I'd had a gun, I may have shot the bastard right then. That is the first time I can ever remember hating my dad for something.

Wes got a 10-speed bicycle for Christmas during the 7th grade but he couldn't use it yet because of the snow on the ground. However, as soon as the weather allowed, he began riding around his neighborhood, then to the edge of the city, then outside of the city. He then reached a major turning point that would change his life forever.

> I spent more and more time away from home, riding my bike all over town. I knew every street and every park in town. I would ride from 30 to 50 miles a day when I was not in school. I was happier when I was exploring. When I was not at home I felt a freedom to do anything I wanted to.

# Chapter 6

## The Pond

About a month before my thirteenth birthday we were living in a duplex. Our landlord was living in the other half. Dad and Mom both worked day shifts and if we had any trouble we could go to the landlord. This gave me a lot of unsupervised time for the first time ever.

*Had you been involved in any of the activities at the school during the seventh grade?*

No, I avoided having any contact with the other kids at school as much as possible. I didn't try out for any of the sports because I was too small and not very coordinated. I felt the other kids laughed at me and didn't want to have anything to do with me.

*How were you able to avoid them during the lunch hour and before and after school?*

I took a school dishwashing job. I didn't get paid but I got a free lunch. I got out of class five minutes early to eat lunch and there were only three of us dishwashers. I got to my first class after lunch five or six minutes late. This meant I totally avoided all the other students during lunch, and only had to deal with them before and after school, or during the five minute breaks between classes.

*Did you have the dishwashing job in the later grades?*

No, but to avoid socializing in the 8th grade I took a job sweeping the hallways at lunchtime. In the 9th grade I worked in the band room, but we'll come to that a little later.

*Okay, let's come back to the summer between the 7th and 8th grades. You were twelve years old when you finished the 7th grade and you turned thirteen on July 3rd. Your parents were working during the day and you were free to do whatever you wanted. What did you do with your time?*

When school got out I had time to ride my bike and explore the entire town of Richland. Within weeks I knew every street in town, every school, every park, every business. I spent up to eight hours a day exploring. I also rode my bike to West Richland, about 3 to 4 miles out, and to Benton City, about 15 miles out, and explored those areas. The Columbia and Yakima rivers bordered these towns. It was desert area all around them. All along the Yakima River were a lot of wooded, bushy areas. I began noticing a lot of areas along both rivers where kids played or fished without adult supervision, but I really had no interest in them at age 12. It's just something I learned, and used a few years later.

*Did you find yourself sexually attracted to any of the kids you saw alone out there by those rivers?*

No, I had no sexual urges yet. The sexual things I had done before this time were not because I was sexually aroused. They were for excitement, probably because I knew they were wrong.

*What about this area? Did it play a part in the progression of your becoming a sex offender?*

I think so, at least to some degree. I was withdrawing from my peers. I still went on camping trips and picnics with my family but I was also withdrawing from them.

*Why were you withdrawing from them now? Were things getting worse at home?*

No, that came a year later. But now, having a bike, I was having fun exploring these areas and it was more fun than being home.

I had known there was a garbage dump outside of town, and one evening, just to get away from the

> family after dinner, I rode my bike out to it, and on the motorbike trails in the desert around it.
>
> I found a small pond between the Yakima River and the dump. The pond was in an isolated area and very few people went there except motorcyclists. I explored the area over the next few days and knew that during the day on weekdays, not even motorcycles were around.
>
> The pond had water from the Yakima River and debris from the garbage dump. And I still had an interest in nudity, but now it was my own body I was interested in. The dirty water didn't matter. I took of all my clothes and jumped in. I loved the thrill of being outside and naked.

A new adventure. A new secret. At first it was very stimulating to him, but he was soon bored with that so he built a raft out of the debris he found in the area and he boldly lay naked on his makeshift raft and floated out into the pond daring anyone to come over the hill and see him. If someone did come, he could easily slip into the water and pull on his swimsuit. He saw this as his greatest accomplishment up to this time.

He had made the raft.

He could outsmart others without getting caught.

He could take risks and get away with it.

He was bold and daring.

He was feeling superior.

By the end of the summer the excitement was almost gone. He attempted to rekindle the excitement by being so daring as to ride his bike all the way around the pond totally nude except for a BB gun in a holster. He was proud of this weapon since he had made the holster himself. His feelings of confidence were growing which superficially served to mask from him his feelings of inferiority. He was now amalgamating sexual excitement with well-planned premeditation and boldness and felt no guilt about it.

*Wes, did you feel that there was anything wrong with what you were doing?*

> No, and I still don't see that there was anything wrong with what I was doing. I wasn't hurting anyone. I wasn't breaking the law. It was fun.

Everything was happening in gradual increments and each step in his pathology was only a small one. He would come to see himself as different, but not abnormal.

He was caught up in the process and it was too enjoyable for him to be willing to step back and take a look at what was happening to him. His activities were secret. Nobody could see the larger picture because he wasn't telling them about it. Each small event that was seen by someone was not viewed in the context of the larger problem.

The human brain at this stage of life is still quite immature. He was still primarily governed by his emotions, and the cognitive abilities that he was developing were used almost solely for the purpose of serving his emotional needs.

Did he have the capability of looking into the future to ascertain possible consequences? That's a question that still needs an answer. What we know is that he had no desire to do so and it's possible that he wouldn't allow himself to consider any consequences even if he did have the capability of doing so. He did know that if his parents or other adults were aware of what he was doing they would have tried to stop it.

All of this was at a pre-masturbation stage. The problem continued to grow. Later, when he was molesting children regularly, a therapist told him that if he didn't change he would possibly kill a child. He was so abhorred by this he didn't go back to this therapist. He likely recognized some truth to the statement.

> I was running around at the pond wearing nothing but the holster. Completely nude. I'd practice "fast draws" and destroying every tin can in sight, when I could actually hit them. now I was outside, naked, not hidden by dirty water, carrying a weapon. My heart pounded like it did the first time I went skinny dipping. Before the excitement of that wore off, 8$^{th}$ grade started and the weather cooled off, so I quit going out to the pond and surrounding area.

That winter, at the age of 13, he discovered masturbation. He soon was stimulating himself once, then twice a day. Since he was lonely and his life was empty of companionship, his chances of becoming addicted to this form of escape were greatly enhanced compared to other kids his age. In his case, masturbation and the fantasy that accompanied it became a deadly addiction that would later lead to his execution.

# Chapter 7

## Turning Point

By the spring of 1975 at the age of 13 I was completely withdrawn from my peers. At home most of my time was spent alone at a bench in the basement or at the desk in my room, building models or reading science fiction and fantasy books.

*You were a good reader?*

Yeah I was. I suppose S.F. and fantasy books were a way to escape, but from what I don't know.

*Do you really not know what you were trying to escape from?*

Not really, no.

*You have been telling me that you were unhappy at home and you were very unhappy at school. When you went to the pond, you felt free and happy and you were comfortable swimming in water that other kids would have avoided. Is it possible that the books you read were an attempt to find in fantasy what you were not finding in reality?*

I guess that's possible.

*How real would the fantasy be for you?*

I could literally put myself into the lead character's body, like the kid in *The Never Ending Story*. It was as if I was actually becoming part of the story. I could almost feel the laser blasts, or the dragon's breath, or whatever. Mom and Dad had to yell to get my attention when I was reading those books.

*You were attempting to live the role of the lead character?*

Yeah.

*What would it do for you? What was it you were after?*

I didn't know then, but I guess it was a substitute for not having friends.

*In* The Never Ending Story *the characters in the book knew the boy was reading about them but he didn't know it. They were trying to get the boy to come to their rescue. Is that what you wanted?*

I guess so.

*You were hoping the kids in school would be friends with you and in turn you would be willing to be of help to them in some way or another.*

    Yeah. I wanted to fit in.

*Since this was only fantasy and it didn't bring you what you were after, you must have been even more disappointed. You would feel something of what you wanted out of life in the books, but it could make you even more aware of what you didn't have in reality. How did you handle that?*

    I ignored my peers, I ignored my family. I kept to myself at home, or just took off on my bike for hours at a time. I never asked permission. I just went. My parents had no idea where I was or what I was doing. I was free. It gave me a certain amount of joy and even pride to be away from home and no one knew where I was. I craved solitude, to be alone with my books, or alone with my sexual thoughts and activities.

*What do you mean by pride?*

    It made me feel grown up. I could make my own decisions and I didn't have to ask anyone for advice, or even for permission. The kids at school made me feel like a failure but these other activities gave me confidence.

*Did working in the band room give you what you were looking for?*

No, I was getting bored with those things. I enjoyed experimenting but I needed something more, something new and exciting.

*I assume you found it.*

In the spring of 1975 I was home alone anywhere from 15 to 30 minutes a couple times a week before my brother, sister, and mother all got home. Because my house's location was near the edge of town, and because of the various school enrollment boundaries, close to half of the elementary school kids walked right past my house on their way home.

My junior high was less than five blocks from my house and it let out 15 minutes earlier than the elementary school. I was home and alone twice a week by the time the younger kids passed my house on their way home.

Where I actually came up with the idea I don't know but I thought it would be exciting to expose myself to children coming home from school.

*Did you have any thought about the possibly of getting caught? After all, you would be exposing yourself from your own house and the kids could tell their parents, or the police, where it happened.*

No, I didn't think about that. It just seemed like it would be something exciting to do.

*What did you do?*

One day while alone I went into my parent's room. I peeked through the curtains waiting for the time when three things happened at once. No traffic or cars coming, no adults or older kids in view, and young kids in view.

*So, this wasn't just an impulsive act. You thought it through. You were planning your strategy in the same way you planned your activities at the pond.*

Yeah. I didn't want anyone but the kids to see me.

*Was this the first time you exposed yourself to anyone?*

Uh huh. I had the window open but the curtains shut. When the time was right, holding the curtains closed with one hand and a finger keeping an eyehole open to watch the kid's reactions, I exposed myself from the waist down. When kids got in front of my house. I yelled, "Hey, look up here! In the upstairs window!"

It worked. I exposed myself to boys and girls, to one child or a group of 5 or 6. It didn't matter because no one reported it.

It was the most exciting thing I'd done so far—my heart was racing, my throat got dry when I saw kids come into sight and no adults in view. The anticipation in the seconds I waited for the kids to get close enough was unbelievably exciting.

*Why do you think that was so exciting?*

Some kids looked and then pointed me out to the other kids. Some boys laughed, telling their friends. Girls might giggle or gasp, then point me out to their friends. There were giggles, laughs. I was pointed at. A couple of times one or two would yell, "Do it again." Once I heard a boy telling some others, "See, that's the window. Wait and see if he does it again." I did.

Not one child ran, or appeared to be scared. Apparently, none of them reported it. Most of them thought it was funny and at least one was showing me to his friends. It was all very encouraging to me. The kids must have felt safe. I wasn't a serious threat to them. They were *outside* on the sidewalk. I was *inside* and *upstairs*.

Wes continued flashing from his bedroom for the next few weeks and still no one reported him. He began to feel that no one would ever report him. On one particular day he exposed himself to a young boy and later that evening a police officer came to his home. The officer stood outside on the front porch talking to his parents. The officer said no charges were being filed but he wanted the adults in the home to know it had occurred.

Possibly thinking the guilty person must have been someone other than their son, Wes's parents told him not to have friends over when they were not home. Nothing more was said of the incident, leaving Wes to feel that his parents didn't care about what had happened, nor did the police since the officer didn't take any names.

I'd been exposing myself over a three to four week period. I'd guess forty or fifty boys and girls ages 6 to 10 saw me during that time. Many seemed to like it, the others just didn't care. Only one reported it. so the kids' reactions were generally encouraging, and I liked doing it. The police scared me, but not enough to stop me. I [eventually] realized my mistake. This was one smart 13 year old.

A strong narcissistic claim. He didn't feel that exposing himself was something that he shouldn't do. His mistake, as he saw it, was that he exposed himself from his own home. He felt that he was smart because he had discovered a treasure and it belonged to him alone. He believed that neither his parents nor the police were concerned enough to take it from him. He felt he could escalate his sexual activities and if he was clever enough he would have fun and not get caught.

This activity had more effect on him becoming a child molester than any single event in his life.

# Chapter 8

## Fallout

Several things were happening at this point. Wes didn't feel any bonding or allegiance to his parents so he didn't feel he had to follow their advice or teachings. He had found sexual activities to be a most exciting, enjoyable, stress-relieving, private, and powerful process and he felt that nobody was concerned enough to question him about it.

His decision was not to change, but only to be more careful in the future. His false sense of power was leading him to narcissistically believe that he was the mastermind of a powerful secret. He was building a pedestal for himself from which he could look down from his self-generated universe to a lesser reality of uninteresting events. To him there was a forty to one chance of not getting caught and he believed that if he was more careful he could stretch this to a hundred to one, or five hundred to one.

I was scared enough to stop for a couple weeks, but by then school was out and kids were no longer walking by every day anyway.

*Did you later continue exposing yourself from the window when you did see a child on the sidewalk?*

No, I felt that even though I hid my face behind the curtain, if a kid did bring a cop to the house, my parents would know for certain that it was me.

*So what did you do that summer?*

With the summer of 1975 upon me, still a bit nervous about the police, I went back to my activities of the previous summer, but things changed a bit. I didn't go back to the pond. It was no longer exciting—it had no appeal left—not after having exposed myself. I went out into the desert, out past the Richland airfield. There were miles of dirt bike trails.

I was getting pretty bold. This summer, to try to put a little excitement back into it, I decided to ride my bike in the desert while nude, except for my shirt. I was approaching age 14 and I usually kept a shirt on when around other people. I didn't want to expose more of my body than necessary. I don't know why. I just wasn't comfortable without a shirt on when I was around others. Too self-conscious, I guess.

*Now, wait a minute. You are planning to ride your bike out in the desert while you're naked but you have to have your shirt on because you're self-conscious? I'm not sure that makes a lot of sense.*

I don't have an explanation for it.

*What would be exciting about riding your bike, or even walking around in the desert with your clothes off, except for your shirt that is? Did you take your clothes off right from the beginning?*

No, I built up to it.

*How do you mean?*

The first couple days in this new area of desert I remained fully clothed, riding my bike and exploring the area, locating possible hiding spots.

*You started out riding fully clothed but you were looking for hiding spots. Why hiding spots?*

I went out there on weekdays when no one was around. Finally, as a practice run I took my shirt off, put it on the rock, and rode my bike around, carefully looking for other people. Calling it a practice run while half naked made it exciting, even though my pants were on. I did no more that first day.

*What was you ultimate purpose?*

It was daring. It gave me a feeling of freedom and power. It was like seeing who could climb highest up a tree.

*I'm not sure I follow that.*

> Every time I did something a little more daring I wanted to see how far I could go with it without getting caught.

The following day Wes returned to the same area in the desert and continued pushing the limits. Even though he didn't like having his shirt off when he was with others, doing so now was daring. First he rode around the area without his shirt. Then he gradually removed other articles of clothing until he felt he could ride out into the desert and back, nude. He planned every sequence in detail to avoid detection and assure success.

> I knew exactly how long it took to get from this ditch to those trees, to that large rock, all possible hiding spots if someone showed up.

He was developing a strategy that was to become a prime directive that would service all of his criminal behaviors in the future.

Planning and rehearsing.

Following his rock and tree adventure he advanced to riding around the desert in only his undershorts. Next he rode his bike around the pond near the landfill totally nude. He then put his clothes on the back of his bike and rode nude two miles out into the desert and back. Next he left his clothes at the starting point, rode nude the two miles into the desert, walked a distance, laid on a rock for a while, and then walked back to his bike, climbed on it, and rode back to his starting point.

He continued with this process whenever he had free time, and with each successful experience his confidence increased and he began to believe that he was smart enough to avoid any detection.

By the end of the summer following the 8th grade, Wes had all the elements in place for his criminal strategy. He might refine his technique in the future but he wouldn't substantially change it.

However, it still wasn't giving him what he wanted. He didn't know what it was that he wanted, he only knew that even with his new activities, he still wasn't finding it.

> But still, it wasn't exciting or dangerous enough. I loved going into the desert and riding my bike or walking in the nude. I continued to get bolder in what I did, but no matter what I tried, I couldn't get back that same feeling I got the first time I'd exposed myself.

During the summer of 1975 Wes noticed that his parents were arguing. It started in their bedroom and began to expand more out in the open and then during picnics and to other activities outside the home.

# Chapter 9

## Ninth Grade

[In my last year of junior high school,] band class was right after lunch, and the room was shared by the choir, so chairs and music stands had to be set-up for band. Wanting to avoid other kids, and really enjoying my 3rd full year of band, as soon as I finished lunch every day I went to the band room. Mr. B gave me the key to the band room, warning me not to let anyone else in—*no problem!*

*What do you mean by no problem?*

This did two things. It kept me away from everyone else, and by setting up chairs and music stands it saved 6 or 7 minutes of valuable time during band class. I liked playing, so the extra time not wasted in class was a benefit to me.

*So this worked quite well for you.*

Occasionally the choir director would come in and play the piano while I worked. He was going over new music he wanted to give one of his classes. I learned there was more to music than just blowing through a mouthpiece. I'd occasionally ask him a question about choir music, and my knowledge of music grew which was another benefit of being in the band room. I could learn instead of acting stupid out in the halls with everyone else at lunchtime.

Mr. B of course quickly learned who had a serious interest in music, and whom he could trust. When he was at lunch I could let certain kids into the band room so they could go into one of the back practice rooms for some extra practice on their instruments. This helped kids who lived in apartments and couldn't practice at home.

*It sounds as if this worked quite well for you.*

Yes, I learned responsibility, I gained the trust of a teacher I admired, and my own knowledge of music increased by listening to the choir director play piano and asking him questions. I like to think that I had a good part in the fact that our band took first place in every contest we went to that year, and maybe buying extra class time for the band did help. It's no wonder, with a man like Mr. B, that I took *great* interest in music.

*So was music important in your life or was it simply a way of escaping, of avoiding the other kids in school?*

[Wes stood up again and walked around the room as if considering how he was going to answer my question. He returned and continued.]

Band then became one of my only two reasons for living. My other reason for living was an ever-increasing desire to reach the level of excitement I had the first time I exposed myself. My entire world was band, sexual activities, and an occasional escape into a good science fiction or fantasy book.

*So you were not considering changing?*

No. The other kids in school had their friends and I wasn't part of any group.

*Were you depressed?*

Not that I remember. I could always find things to do.

During the remainder of the 9th grade Wes continued to hide out from his peers by staying in the band room as often as possible. The band director, not understanding the primary reason for this, was impressed at his seeming interest in music. A door was opening for a music career.

At the end of the school year, I was given two awards, one for being the best musician in the band, and a director's award which was given to the person who did the most to help the band.

*Help in what way?*

Like the most inspiring, the hardest worker in the band, or the best volunteer. The awards were to be given at a potluck picnic for band members and their families at a local park. My parents didn't come. Dad and Mom were arguing more with each other and it was obvious that Dad and Mom would not stay together.

# Chapter 10

## The Next Step

I was 14 years old when I took the next step in my sexual activities. Skinny dipping was no longer exciting. Exposing myself was great but it got boring after a while. Riding the bike nude was becoming boring. I needed something new to keep the excitement going. I wanted to do something sexual. I agreed to go to a relative's house with the family for a barbeque thinking that maybe it would take my mind off things. I had a 9 year old cousin who mentioned a carnival game in which you could put your hand in a box and attempt to identify the object in there. If you were able to do it, you would win a prize.

It gave me an idea. I enticed my cousin to come into the dark closet with me and I would put something in her hand to see if she could identify it.

Wes had her handle his genitals. She allowed him to touch her genital area as well. When his brother and sister came into the room, Wes got them to watch him and his cousin do it again. His brother allowed Wes to do it to him but his sister didn't.

It was the first time I'd ever molested anyone. I molested a 9-year old girl twice, and a 6-year old boy all in one day. Neither of them reported it.

I continued trying to get my sister to play the guessing game after that but she wouldn't. She just wasn't interested, but I didn't give up. I attempted to touch her when she was asleep but she woke up. I never attempted to molest her after that.

*It sounds like you were proud of these sexual achievements.*

Yeah, I was.

*Was it that you felt like a failure in your social life at school so in contrast these small conquests were very big to you?*

I felt that if I could get them to enjoy it then we could enjoy it together.

*So, it wasn't just a sexual experience, it was a need for companionship of some sort. Wes, what about your family? Did they stay together?"*

No. I can't remember exactly which day word of the divorce came, but I know Mom and Dad hadn't intended to tell us, but my sister overheard them talking. My 15th birthday was July 3, 1976. News of the divorce came on either July 2nd or 3rd, I don't remember which. The next morning, Mom told us she was taking Dad to the mental hospital. He'd tried to kill himself. Again, I don't remember which day it happened, but the divorce was one day and the suicide attempt the next day and one of them was on my 15th birthday. What sticks in my mind is, "Happy birthday, your dad just tried to kill himself."

*That must have been traumatic for you and Amber and Gary.*

Amber and Gary cried, but how did I feel about the suicide attempt? I didn't care. I have never had any love for him or anyone else in my family. It was a happy childhood, but it was more of a "roommate" situation than a family. Only rarely, in my very early childhood, did I ever see Mom and Dad hug each other, and seeing them kiss was a major news headline. And not once ever did I hear either of them say "I love you." They didn't say it to each other and they didn't say it to us kids. My response to Dad's attempted suicide was, "It figures. No big deal. He couldn't even kill himself right!"

We went to visit Dad at the mental hospital. I didn't want to go. What if someone saw me there and thought there was something wrong with *me*?

It brought to mind the time my father had a heart attack. I was working in another city from where Dad was located. I rushed down to the hospital so fast that I clipped a deer running across the highway. It stunned me that Wes had no love or compassion towards his father. It was hard for me to understand how cold-hearted Westley Dodd had become by this time in his life. But then, it helped me understand his total lack of compassion for his future victims.

*Did your father's suicide attempt have any effect on your life?*

No, not really. He got out of the hospital and got him[self] an apartment. I decided to continue exposing myself, but I'd do it from somewhere other than my own home. That way, no one would know where to send the police if they reported me. On some days, while wearing blue jeans and a T-shirt, I exposed myself on impulse. I was 15, exposing to anyone under age ten.

One day Wes saw four young boys playing in a front yard. He stopped and asked them to come over to him and he exposed himself. He had advanced from jeans to gym shorts because he could carry out the act and get away quicker. After exposing himself he quickly rode off on his bike.

Normally, after exposing myself, I immediately left the area and avoided it for several days, in case I was reported. But for some reason, I don't really don't know, I rode back around the block, tucking my genitals back into my shorts. When I got back around to the corner of the street the boys were on, they saw me and yelled, "Do it again."

I looked around to make sure no adults were around, and rode up to them, stopping on the sidewalk in front of the house they were at. They walked over to me and I asked if they really wanted me to do it again. I was already formulating a plan. I was bored with exposing myself. It was no longer exciting. I said I would if one of them did it first. One boy who was four or five years old said, "I will," and right there on the sidewalk he unsnapped and unzipped his pants, pulling them down in front.

We were on the sidewalk in the center of a residential street with houses on both sides of the house the kids were at, and several in view across the street. I wanted more privacy and my trained eye had already spotted just the right place.

He had the boys follow him to the side of one of the houses where there were shrubs to hide behind. Wes exposed himself and asked if one of the boys wanted to touch it. One of the younger boys said he would and when he touched Wes, he said, "Yup. It's real." The other boys laughed. Once more, Wes was encouraged by their reaction. The boys said they would meet him at a school a couple blocks down the road that afternoon. He was planning further sexual activities with them but the boys didn't show up.

At this point, Wes had become almost incapable of feeling empathy. He was totally self-focused. He had become a psychopath by the age of 15.

Wes's behavior makes particular sense when looking through his eyes at the comparative manner in which he perceived his place within his teen world. The 7th and 8th grades are a time for dances, choosing friends, increased social life, and sports. There is a discovery of the opposite sex, a strong interest in clothing styles, and greater attention is paid to characteristics that make one accepted. There is a strong need to be part of something. Wes had none of this. His social skills were underdeveloped. The world was moving forward but Wes was being left behind, and the more he got behind the more alienated he felt.

In the 9th and 10th grades boys start coming into their own. There is an even greater interest in girls. The youth fall into specific groups and the "in" groups are starting to solidify. The inferior are shunned and the popular are sought out. Above all else, a person must have at least one friend so as not to be a complete loner or to appear weird. Wes had none.

He was in an existential void. His vision for his future had narrowed to encompass only the fulfilling of his pathology. Marriage and a family were out of the question. He disliked himself but this self-perception was intolerable so he compartmentalized it. He locked it behind thick iron walls deep in his mind. Guilt was not an emotion he would allow himself to feel. Or, perhaps, he was incapable of feeling it.

There were no role models that he could identify with. He would never again allow himself to be the subject of close scrutiny and ridicule as had happened years before in the PE locker room, and he wouldn't talk to anyone about his problem because he believed they wouldn't understand and they would call him evil and sick. Some of the kids in school were experimenting with drugs and alcohol. Wes avoided these.

He was dichotomizing into what psychiatrist Carl Jung referred to as a Persona and a Shadow, a normal-appearing self and a conniving self which he kept hidden. His well-manicured Persona would entice others into believing that he was an upstanding citizen and this would allow him to hide the Shadow—the dark side, the evil side. By now, the Shadow was almost fully developed.

Wes couldn't return to "normal" thinking because he hadn't engaged in such a process since he was a child. He was no longer aware of what normal thinking was. Emotionally, Wes had fixated at a childhood level and unless he made a conscious decision to change he would never advance in maturity beyond this point.

He was socially and emotionally totally alone. The sexual fantasies and activities were not simply for sexual gratification. Sex was the vehicle to friendship, admiration, and approval. However relationships with other youth his age was by now out of the question. He was very lonely and needed a relationship with someone. Children were the only ones who showed an interest in him and he believed this was because he was exposing himself to them.

*Wes, what was your fantasy life at this point? I remember you telling me that you had an active one.*

> As I got older, I fantasized about actually being a hero when I wasn't fantasizing about molesting children. I daydreamed about being a member of a mountain search and rescue team, and in those daydreams we were always rescuing children. Why it was always children? I'm not sure. Me and my team would find a lost or an injured child, and I'd comfort him or her. I would feed the child, hold their hand, and when broken bones were being set, I'd help calm the child. I might be fantasizing about molesting a boy or girl, then a few minutes later I'd be daydreaming about rescuing a child from a cliff face, everyone patting me on the back telling me what a good job I'd done. But then in a few more minutes I'd be thinking about molesting [a] child again.

Wes wanted to be accepted and admired and he had hero fantasies in which he was doing great things for injured children. However, the chance of helping someone was extremely remote, so his fantasies turned to obtaining closeness through sex. It was a poor substitute but Wes believed there was no other alternative that would work for him.

# Chapter 11

## First Arrest

Inevitably the time came when Wes was caught and arrested and had to go to court. There had been many sexual occurrences but he confessed to only seven accounts of Indecent Exposure. Since he seemed cooperative and since this was his first arrest the charges were dropped. The second arrest came later when a girl reported him to the police. The third came less than six months later on March 10th, 1977 at the age of 15. He was required to go to therapy, which he did. He minimized his sexual activities and overplayed the effect of his parent's divorce and his father's suicide attempt. Wes commented, "I did not tell him about all the sex-related things I'd done prior to the divorce."

On the positive side, Wes was still in band and liked his band instructor. His group took first place in a state-wide competition and Wes seriously considered a career in music. He was asked to student teach the beginning band [class] and was encouraged to learn other instruments in anticipation of a college education. Wes said, "I liked being able to teach others what I myself enjoyed so much. I just plain had fun." More people were giving him recognition for his talents.

### The 12$^{th}$ grade

During his senior year he focused on music and creative writing. He studied music therapy at the college level and learned to arrange music. He was often put in charge when either of the band directors had to be gone. He wrote a musical composition and the band played it. He taught music and was allowed to lead the band at performances. He was being groomed to become a music teacher and he was told that with his experience he could probably skip the college freshman music classes.

> I was definitely a leader in our high school band. I was always a driving force in fund-raisers and always involved when the band ran a concession stand at ball games, taking charge of the set-up and cleanup crews. On trips I always ended up in charge of loading and unloading gear from the buses and truck[s].

Regarding his sexual activities during this time, neither the arrest nor his musical accomplishments slowed him down. Some very positive things were happening in his life but he had already become too addicted to want to stop.

But addicted to what?

It was not so much for the sex as it was for the lifestyle that went with it. He had contact with kids, he felt that some of them were friendly towards him, he was outsmarting the police, and he had a secret life which to him was a very exciting adventure.

> I confessed to several crimes, but only one thing was obvious. The police didn't care about them. I was charged with only one of seven known crimes, and that charge was dropped. Another obvious point was that I had not been reported at all for any of my more serious crimes, and even several exposure crimes had gone unreported. The overall reaction of the kids was very encouraging. There was a very good chance that my crimes would continue to go unreported, and even if they were reported I would never be prosecuted. I liked it, the kids liked it (apparently), and the police didn't care.

His greatest fulfillment was not through his initial engagement with a child, but through his fantasies after. He first flashed to children. Next he got a child to touch him (or to touch the child). Then he would go home and masturbate to the memory of the contact. He soon advanced to the point where he would put his mouth on a boy's penis for a very short time and then return home. For years there was no on-site masturbation of himself or of the child when he was with the child. His sexual interaction with the child was to provide him with visual imagery that he would use later in a lengthy sexual fantasy between himself and the child that he had just molested.

During the summer of 1977 (age 15 to 16), Wes continued with his sexual activities. With each event he would add something new to make the act more daring than his previous exploits had been.

> I continued with all my "lonely activities" at home, but I got more daring. I no longer went into the desert outside of town to walk or ride my bike in the nude. I did it in town in full view of several houses. I had very little fear of getting caught.

Wes watched for any opportunity to expose himself to kids and was successful at finding boys who would watch him, and on at least one occasion a couple of boys asked him to do it again. These activities continued beyond his graduation from high school.

In September, 1981, Wes joined the Navy. He continued to get involved with molesting children while there, and in July of 1982 he was arrested for Unauthorized Absence and was given an Administrative Discharge in November or December of that same year.

# Chapter 12

## Richie and Sammy

In 1987, Wes was living in Kennewick with a married couple who had a four year old child named Richie. Wes, being very lonely, quickly got attached to the boy. Once he began molesting the boy he continued doing so almost daily for five months. This temporarily satisfied Wes's need for companionship but he had no regard for what he was doing to the boy. After the boy told his parents of the sexual abuse for the third time, Wes decided he should move out before they reported it to the police. Wes had become very attached to this boy and it was very difficult for to leave him. Richie had been his friend. His lover. Wes was not lonely when he was with Richie. Still, he thought there would be less chance Richie's parents would report him if he wasn't living there, so he moved out. The closeness he felt with the boy would affect him for the rest of his life. Wes needed love and he believed it could only come from a child.

He went to Seattle and stayed with his sister. Her boyfriend, Ralph, and his two-year-old son, Sammy, were there as well. Wes greatly missed the companionship and easy molestation of Richie and Sammy became an exciting challenge for him. Wes was desperate for companionship. However, he also used this as an excuse to escalate the intensity of his activities. He decided that if he couldn't get the sex willingly, he would take it. He failed to recognize it was companionship that he really wanted and that sexual contact was a very incomplete substitute. Also, he was aware of his chances of getting caught so he decided he would have to make each engagement worth the risk.

> If I was going to find kids I didn't know—kids who couldn't identify me as easily as Richie could have—then I would not only do oral sex on whoever I found, but simulate intercourse as well. I would not give any kid a choice as I had years before when I molested kids I found in parks or at schools. If I found any child in an area out of sight of everyone else, that child would submit to my desires. I really missed Richie. I would not accept "no" from any child.

Wes forced Sammy to engage in a sexual activity with him in spite of the fact that the child was crying.

> This was the first time I had ever used physical force… I couldn't believe I had allowed myself to lose control like that. I felt sorry for Sammy, and did all I could to cheer him up. BUT… during that struggle, during my first use of force, I experienced the strongest climax I had ever had—it was also the fastest. The struggle was very stimulating… and so powerful, that was all I could think of… and I knew I would try to again reach that level. I was now a rapist. No longer would I take a no or physical resistance as an answer. It would be easier if the child cooperated, or at least submitted, but it would be more stimulating if there was a struggle. I didn't know it then, but wanting some kids to struggle was the next to the last step to murder. On the "negative" side, I realized that, during the assault, I had become completely oblivious to my surroundings—something that could get me caught in the future if I wasn't careful. But all was well, and I learned from the experience in the safety of my own home.

A marked change in Wes's identity occurred and he was one step closer to being able to visualize himself as a killer. He had crossed over a line from sick to evil.

# Chapter 13

## Considering Homicide

Ralph changed jobs and he and Sammy moved shortly after the rape of the boy. Again, Wes was lonely and depressed. He was forced to go back to the parks and school grounds to look for victims. He wanted his own child. One to live with him. He was tired of the brief encounters. His dilemma was of what to do with a child if he got tired of him. The only way to prevent a child from reporting him to the police was to kill him.

This thought was not repulsive to Wes because he had found so much exhilaration in the child's struggle while he raped him. He started actively considering molesting and then killing a child to avoid detection. However, he wasn't sure if he could actually kill another human being. His fear wasn't of getting caught, but of whether or not he could bring himself to follow through on a designated plan. He decided he had to condition himself to kill. But how?

> I still wasn't sure about being able to kill, but with killing in mind, I became sexually aroused as I fantasized about the sexual assault itself. Killing started becoming associated with my sexual arousal. If I could make the thoughts of murder itself as exciting as the rape, then I would be able to follow through with it. I fantasized about them struggling, causing me to have a very powerful climax. I just took it a step further. As best as I can recall, I fantasized about killing for only a week or so before I was sure I could actually take a child's life. All I had to do was wait for the opportunity.

His first thought of killing a child came about four months after raping Sammy. He focused his attention on ways to find kids. He drew maps of neighborhoods and parks. He looked for places where he might find kids alone on weekends or during the summer. When he found a spot that looked good he would circle it in green on his map and he would make notes in black ink. In particular, he liked newer housing areas that were close to parks or wooded areas.

On the morning of Saturday, June 13, 1987, about two weeks following his first thoughts of murder, he made his final preparations. He had a "murder kit" in a briefcase consisting of various sizes of rope, an Ace bandage, a pocketknife, and a fish fillet knife. He considered every possible victim problem and rehearsed every security precaution that would allow him to avoid detection. He went over every scenario he could think of relative to the act until he thoroughly believed he could carry it out and not get caught.

He didn't care if his victim was a boy or a girl. Either would do.

His primary objective was to prove to himself that he could kill a child. If he could carry through, he could then expand his range of activities considerably.

He drove to a school and watched the playground for children. At first there were two, but they soon left the area. Then three more boys came. Wes decided on his divide and conquer scheme and he approached the three boys telling them he was looking for a young boy named Jimmy and needed their help to find him. They agreed. When he said he wanted one of them to ride with him while the other two searched the woods, they turned him down, saying the three of them would search the woods for the boy and if they found him they would bring him to the playground. He thanked them and quickly returned to his car to get out of there before they reported him as a suspicious person.

He was frustrated but not willing to give up. He remembered Mike, a six year old boy living at a motel next to a construction site where Wes was then working as a security guard. He believed that Mike trusted him because Wes had bandaged an injured ankle for him. When he arrived at the construction site, Mike and some friends were playing on a pile of dirt. Wes called him over and asked if he would go with him to locate a child that was lost. Mike agreed and said he would get his other friends to come as well. At this point Wes saw two construction workers who could identify him drive onto the site. He got scared and drove off. Heading back towards the school he got a flat and didn't have a spare so he hitchhiked home to get some money to get the flat fixed. Mike informed his parents about what had happened and they notified the police. Wes was identified by the construction workers. He was arrested for Attempted Unlawful Detainment. He served 118 days in the King County Jail, was given a one year probation with required counseling, and was prohibited from having any contact with children.

Wes made the decision to not change. Instead, he would be more careful.

> I had tried, failed, and got caught. I'd also gotten away with attempted murder. I analyzed my mistakes and learned. If I tried to abduct a child in the future, I would at least have sense to not try to abduct a kid that *knew* where I worked. I'd also be more careful in other areas and have more specific rape and murder plans ahead of time. That 118 days in jail did nothing but teach me to be more exact in my planning and more cautious in my selection of abduction sites and my approaches to children.

After serving his jail time, Wes at first stayed with his father in Vancouver and began looking for a counseling program as required. Then he got an apartment in Renton with his sister and her boyfriend. He failed to contact the probation officer (PO) who had been assigned to him after his jail time in Seattle. His PO called and asked why Wes hadn't checked in. Wes was given 24 hours to report in or he would be sent back to jail.

His sister, Amber, and her new boyfriend, Ron, were living in Wes's apartment in Renton. Wes's probation officer gave a stipulation that Wes was not allowed to have any contact with children. Wes heard that Ralph and his son Sammy were back in town. Sammy was just under three years of age. Amber and her boyfriend left, Ralph and Sammy moved in, and Wes didn't tell his probation officer that Sammy was there.

Wes was evaluated by Dr. Von Kline on November 17, 1987 for possible inclusion in his sex offender program.

> A 10-minute walk put me in the heart of two different shopping centers in downtown Renton. I saw a convenience store I liked that had a help wanted sign. I was working the next night. Getting a job has never been a problem. I've never put in more than one job application, and was never unemployed longer than three days, unless it was by choice.
>
> I had my first paycheck in time for Thanksgiving, 1987. I had a lot to be thankful for! My PO

was happy, Dr. Von Kline had accepted me into his program, I had a job I really liked, and my boss was impressed with my speed, skill, and experience. Amber and Ron were gone, and it was just me, Ralph, and Sammy in a relaxed, happy home."

Ralph was poor and he and Sammy had lived in poverty circumstances so Sammy hadn't eaten very well. Wes prepared an eight or nine course meal for Ralph and Sammy, but it primarily for Sammy. Wes referred to Sammy as "my nephew" and said, "He'd never had a decent Thanksgiving meal. Sammy helped me, and couldn't believe it! He'd never seen so much food! Us 'three bachelors' were doing good."

Wes was happy now because he had Sammy. He got along well with Ralph, and Sammy didn't seem to recognize Wes so the boy didn't demonstrate any fear of him.

However, there were two problems at this point. First, Wes was violating his probation stipulation to not have contact with children. Second, Ralph got a night job working in a mill. His shift started at 5:00 pm and he got home at 4:00 am the next morning. Wes worked at the store Monday through Friday from 2:00 p.m. to 10:00 pm but his boss would give him extra time off, or would change shifts with him. Ralph would drop his son off at a childcare center on his way to work and would pick him up after his shift ended. Wes offered to save Ralph money by taking care of Sammy at specific times when he was off work and Ralph was still working.

He attempted to molest Sammy one evening when Ralph was at work. It had been 10 months since Wes had had a victim, and his last victim was Sammy. Sammy still couldn't talk and he would turn age three tomorrow. Wes was able to get him laughing as he prepared to molest him. However, Sammy began to remember Wes and the prior trauma and he resisted, which caused Wes to reach climax.

Wes was making a cake for Sammy's birthday and he didn't have frosting for it. He took Sammy to the store, bought a few things, returned home, frosted the cake, and played with Sammy for a while. He put the boy to bed and when he was sure the boy was asleep, he went in and molested him again. Sammy woke up and struggled. Wes said, "He didn't scream, but he cried a little. I didn't care. He'd learn to accept this as a way of life. I covered him up and went to bed."

His next chance to molest Sammy was on New Year's Eve. Ralph wanted to go out for the night and be with his friends and Wes said that he would babysit Sammy.

He had first checked with his PO on November 9, 1987 and started treatment with Dr. Von Kline on November 17, 1987. Wes had raped Sammy three times in just a few weeks.

> Three new felonies in the first two months of my probation. The court didn't slow me down, my PO and counselor didn't bother me. In fact, they both thought I was being very cooperative. I gave Dr. Von Kline a very long summary of my previ-

ous crimes, both reported and unreported. Dr. Von Kline reported to my PO. My PO was apparently impressed with my honesty and openness and thought he could trust me. He was also a regular customer of mine at the Shell station convenience store I worked at. He saw me quite a bit outside of regular monthly office visits, so [he] never came to my apartment. I never gave my PO or Von Kline reason to suspect a child lived with me.

Wes talked in therapy about the boy he had attempted to kidnap from the construction area in Seattle, saying that he was going to molest the boy. That was all.

I had revealed a lot of previously unknown stuff, but kept a lot hidden. I was in violation of probation just being around Sammy, and I raped him three times in just a two week period, and still had 10 months of probation left. In counseling, I complained about work, money, the poorly running pickup I had bought, anything to avoid the real reason I was there. I just did what I had to do to stay out of jail so I could continue raping Sammy and finally make him a willing sex partner, or at least submissive.

Wes began spending a lot more time with Sammy. He would take Sammy to the store with him, he took him to McDonalds, he watched cartoons with him, he played with him. The boy got used to sexual play. Wes took Polaroid pictures of the boy to use in his solitary sexual activities. He was able to make the boy laugh and it soon reached the point that the boy came to him to play. Wes made the sexual activities with Sammy appear to be part of a game, including tickling and laughter. He began to think of Sammy as a sexual partner rather than a victim.

> I wanted Sammy to like it so he'd let me do it again. But I loved Sammy as any uncle would love a nephew, a normal child kind of love. And now, he was letting me do anything I wanted. I was now gentle instead of forceful. Sammy was cooperative and willing to let me do anything, which no other boy had done.
>
> I started having new feelings for Sammy. I still loved him the normal way, but now I didn't just want my own sexual gratification, I started feeling like I didn't want to molest Sammy, but I wanted to make love to him. I had some real sexual feelings for him, and now, for the first time, I wanted a little boy to enjoy the same feelings. I now wanted a sex partner not just for my own pleasure, but for both of us.

My thoughts about this were: Wes, you've got to be kidding. How in God's name could you think that a three year old boy could become your sexual partner? Did you not consider the fact that you were destroying the boy's life?

I realized that Wes had corrupted his thinking so severely that it was probably impossible at this point for him to truly believe that what he was doing to the child was wrong. His rationale was that he could make it fun for the boy, that the boy would laugh rather than cry when they were sexually engaged, that the boy's father wasn't aware of it, nor was his probation officer or his therapist, and that the boy still couldn't talk so he was unable to tell his father what was happening to him.

Wes molested Sammy three times in one evening.

> The first time this night it was having sex and, by the third time, it had become making love, and I just couldn't get enough of my lover. I couldn't get over it. I never imagined that I'd have anything other than a victim, or maybe a willing partner if I was lucky. I had developed real sexual feelings for Sammy.

Wes was considering a lifetime arrangement.

> I believed that his own sexual feelings would awaken. By the time he was 10 he'd be an absolutely perfect lover for me. He'd learn how to please me, rather than just lay motionless. I'd train my lover right.
>
> I went to bed. In the morning I was dreaming about making love to Sammy. I had never dreamed about a child that way before. Wasn't there a say-

ing about knowing it was true love if you dreamed about the other person?

Was it really love, or was it just lust? I did care about Sammy. I loved him in all the normal, healthy ways a man loves a child. Was I just combining the healthy love with the sexual desire? I decided it didn't matter. I had a willing sex partner. That was the important thing.

I don't know what became of Sammy. It was later learned that he was partially deaf and this was the reason he wasn't learning to talk. I can't believe the boy grew into adulthood in a normal fashion without severe psychological problems.

Wes continued his sexual activities with Sammy for three weeks and on Friday, February 5, 1988, Ralph's ex-wife came for a visit. Wes had gone to work. Around noon, his PO called to check on him. While talking to Ralph's ex-wife he heard Sammy's voice in the background. The PO called Wes at work and ordered him to move out of the house that day. Wes got a two bedroom apartment 3 or 4 blocks from where he was working.

> My PO and Dr. Von Kline talked. Child Protective Services (CPS) went to interview Sammy. Of course, he couldn't tell them anything. My next session with Dr. Von Kline was Monday, February 8, 1988. He told me I was to take a polygraph the following Saturday. The key questions were: 1) Did

I molest Sammy? 2) Did I have thoughts of molesting Sammy? 3) Had I molested, or had thoughts of molesting any other children?

I had six days to make myself believe the answers to all three questions were *no!* I passed the polygraph, and nothing else was said. My PO seemed satisfied. It was a close call, but I'd gotten away with it. Fortunately, no one looked into my briefcase and found those photos I'd taken of Sammy. I used those photos daily, sometimes twice daily, and masturbated. I missed Sammy bad and now he had been taken away from me.

*How did you handle it?*

In my apartment, alone, lonely and bored, the old thoughts of murder came back. I also started having some new thoughts. I had been satisfied with Sammy and I didn't want to take any risks that I would jeopardize my relationship with him, so while I had him, I didn't look for other kids, and had no desire to murder. I was concerned about losing access to Sammy so I didn't even look for others. But now that my living arrangements weren't themselves a probation violation, I could begin taking small chances once in a while.

*You said you started having some new thoughts as well. What new thoughts?*

I had just bought a VCR and there was a store a couple of blocks away that rented tapes. Perhaps I could lure a kid home to watch a movie. The store attracted a lot of neighborhood kids, as it had several video games. Perhaps a kid would come into my store as I was getting ready to close and would agree to help me close the store and follow me to my apartment next door. I would rape a boy or girl and no one would be close enough to hear their screams. I could kill him/her/them, and dump the body in an alleyway garbage dumpster downtown. I'd keep myself open to all possibilities, but I would not actively search for a child while I was still on probation.

I met my PO on March 8, 1988. According to his log there were no problems. He wasn't in his office at my next appointment in April, and his secretary said I could just fill out the standard monthly paperwork and I'd be good until the next month. He saw me at work when he bought gas for his car in April and in May.

I had been promoted and transferred to a different store. I wanted my PO to know every change in my work or home. I would not take a chance of him finding out about a change before my next appointment with him and him thinking I was hiding it for some reason. The instant I learned of my promotion and transfer, I went straight to his office.

It was now May of 1988. Wes was working towards getting off probation but he was beginning to consider

## The Case of Westley Allan Dodd

homicide again. In a little over a year from now, Westley Dodd would kill two boys as part of an "experiment" to determine if he could actually do it. He had learned from the polygraph experience that he could control his emotional responses if he trained himself to do so. Maybe, he thought, he could condition himself to be able to kill a child.

> There was a bookstore across the street from my apartment, and while looking around one day I saw a book about the Occult and read the back cover. I don't remember now, but the book was something about the practices of various cults, and the back cover talked about a ceremony in which children were molested by adults—parents molesting their own children first, then this boy and another child had to throw darts at a baby before the baby was sacrificed. I didn't have any money for the book, and when I went back a couple of days later, I couldn't find it.

*Did you give up that idea for now?*

> No. I thought that maybe I could start my own occult group. As the leader I'd have access to everyone's kids and I could rape whatever child was to be sacrificed in private, and of course I'd be there to kill the child in the ceremony.
>
> I decided that was just too much, even for me. But what if there was really something to all that satanic stuff? Was Satan real? Would Satan help me

gain access to children? I had a two bedroom apartment all to myself. One room was empty except for my desk. I can't remember now what I called the room, but it had something to do with nude children.

I got a cardboard box from work and drew a pentagram on it. Then I poked several holes on the drawing on the box, and from behind I took a string of miniature Christmas lights, all red, and pushed them through the holes. When I plugged it in. That gave me an imitation of a flaming pentagram. I sat the pentagram on my desk. I added a second light switch in the room to control the electrical outlets. I bought a red light at the store and put in a lamp at the back of the room.

Wes put a string of candles on the floor below the pentagram on his desk. He put Sammy's pictures in front of the candles and sat in front of them. He would leave the room, undress and re-enter the room. It was all dark except the string of lights and the candles. He would tell Satan he wanted Sammy back, or a boy like him "that I could keep.

Since his sister and her boyfriend might come by unexpectedly, Wes would take down this set-up when he finished so no one would see it. After trying it a few times he decided it wasn't going to work so he got rid of it.

Wes was a good worker and the customers of the convenience store in which he worked were impressed with him, as was the manager. He was soon made manager of a sister store. He loved the challenge: "It was the funnest time I'd had in a long time."

Within two weeks the manager of a partner store quit so Wes was given the responsibility of running both stores. He wanted to work his way up to managing three or four of them. It was a possible new beginning for him, but he still had the sense of being inferior, a problem which had plagued him when he was asked to direct the band in high school. Through his work he had chances for a social life but he rejected them.

> As time went on, I began moving more and more and never stayed in one job for more than a year before getting tired of it and moving on, so that didn't help either. At the same time, my sexual urges were getting stronger, and if I knew of a good place, I preferred to go look for children rather than go to a friend's house. I ended up in jobs where there weren't many people around, so I never met anyone new. At the same time, I spent less and less time with the friends I had and more time molesting. By the time I got to Vancouver, even though I got along with my coworkers, I refused several invitations for weekend fishing or camping trips, nor did I go to restaurants with the crew when asked. I devoted all my time to planning crimes and looking for children. I had no time for friends.

# Chapter 14

### Cassie

In May of 1988, Wes was promoted manager of one of the two stores he was working at. Ralph didn't have a place to live that was close to his work so Wes invited him to come and stay in his apartment. He did, and his ex-wife stopped by overnight on her way to Idaho. Sammy crawled in bed with Wes the next morning and Wes molested him. Sammy and his mother then left. Someone reported to Wes's PO that Sammy was in the apartment. His PO checked but Sammy was gone by then.

Ralph's former girlfriend, Ruth, came to stay during the middle of June, 1988, just a couple of days after Sammy had been there. Ruth's daughter Cassie, who was Wes's age, came the next day.

The three of us picked Cassie up at the bus station that morning. I had to work [the] swing shift that day. When we got home, Cassie said she'd buy me lunch if I gave her a ride to Arby's.

I don't recall feeling attracted to her in any way, but still, it sounded like a lunch date. It couldn't hurt to give her a ride and a free lunch was hard to pass up. I have no idea who said it, but it came out of my mouth, but I was never brave enough to say something like this, but I suggested taking our lunch to a nearby park where we could feed the ducks. It just seemed like the thing to say at the time. Normally, I'd be too afraid of rejection and embarrassment, but it just spilled out.

We went to the park, ate, talked, fed the ducks, then as we walked back to my pickup, I thought: Should I? Will she let me? Dare I? I reached down and thought, "Oh, just take it, chicken!" I took her hand. No problem! Her hand closed on mine. *Wahoo!* I couldn't believe it. Look at me, world! I have a girlfriend! Who would have ever thought I would have a girlfriend! I wanted everyone to see me with her. It didn't matter that she was a bit overweight. I might not be envied by other men, but damn, I felt great and didn't care what others thought. That was new. I used to always worry about what the guys would think of me if I couldn't get the beautiful ones. But I didn't care now.

I really don't know what happened. Just three or four days earlier I was in bed with my three and a half year old lover boy and that was all that mattered. Now I'd forgotten about Sammy. Cassie had initiated this by inviting ME to lunch. I didn't have to take the first step myself. Maybe that's why it was so easy for me.

She sat in the center of the seat of my pickup, right next to me, on the way home. I had even opened the door for her. What was happening to me?

I got ready for work and she walked me out to my pickup. I didn't expect her next move. She put her hands on my waist and kissed me! She kissed me! It was my first kiss. Then she said to hurry home and she turned and went back inside. Hurry home? As I drove to work I thought, *Oh boy, I'm going to get some tonight.* I don't know why I thought that. It must have been because she was the aggressive one. She was the one risking rejection.

I found it easy to think about going to bed with her. I *expected* to go to bed with her when I got home. I'd seen other women I'd like to date and sleep with but was always afraid they'd say and think I was crazy or something. I wanted to, but never expected it like I did now.

I got home. We all talked a while. Ralph and Ruth went to bed and Cassie and I sat next to each other watching TV. I got up to go to bed. I wanted sex and I was sure that she wanted it also, but yet I didn't ask her into my room. She had a bed made up on the couch.

Wes retired to his room but Cassie soon came to his room asking to sleep on the floor in her sleeping bag. Wes invited her into his bed. She said she was married but separated. Since she was honest Wes decided to be truthful as well so he told her he was on probation for molesting a child. She didn't care. She told him she was involved in witchcraft. Wes didn't care. They made love.

> If she got pregnant, well, I love kids. I had always wanted a son, not to molest, but I did daydream about having a family, playing baseball with the boys or building dollhouses for the girls. I just never expected it to become reality, especially when I looked for children instead of women to have sex with.

Wes told his therapist about Cassie and it angered him when his therapist discouraged the relationship and suggested that he should seek out an adult homosexual relationship instead. Wes wrote, "Both my PO and my counselor seemed to forget that my record clearly showed just as many female victims as males."

> I wanted to change. With Cassie, my desires to molest were all but completely gone. I had opportunities to molest a couple of times but didn't because I was satisfied with Cassie.

However, this would not be true for very long. Wes wrote in a later letter that his therapist was right in suggesting a homosexual relationship. With Cassie having just come into his life, Wes was excited about it. He enjoyed the sex with Cassie and he thought that his days of molesting children were likely over. However, his sexual preferences and habits were too ingrained for the possibility of a quick change. Cassie had two children, Robert who was one year old and Beverly who was two years old. He said regarding Robert,

> I'd have one last fling before marrying Cassie and becoming a normal father and husband.

They had talked about getting married. Cassie told Wes that she would get a U-Haul and bring her things from her other residence to his place. She would take Beverly and leave Robert with Wes. Wes was excited about this and planned on molesting Robert just this once while she was gone.

Cassie changed her mind at the last minute and took Robert and left Beverly. Wes considered molesting Beverly but she fussed too much when he attempted to change her diaper.

The next morning, Cassie returned with an empty U-Haul and collected her things and her child and left without giving Wes an explanation. When it had seemed that he and Cassie would be getting married, Wes threw all of his pictures of Sammy and other children in the trash. When Cassie left, he got them all out again. He told his counselor about her leaving, and his counselor seemed pleased that they weren't getting married.

The relationship had lasted one month.

He was angry and depressed and began considering homicide again. Still, he didn't want others to detect this evil side of him and tried to hide it just in case someone might become suspicious. His persona had to be perfect so that if he was suspected of abducting a child, no one would believe it.

> I would save a life if I could, but not because it felt good—but because it made me look good. If I were to save somebody's life, I would never come close to being a suspect when a child disappeared.

Wes, Ruth, and Ralph moved from the crowded two bedroom apartment into a house, and Sammy returned. Wes no longer considered marriage, or even simply molesting children. Those sexual engagements were no longer exciting. He was angry at people, at the world, and at life. He had no friends except Ralph and Ruth, and they weren't really friends in the true sense. He had only Sammy. However, this relationship didn't satisfy his anger and his need for control. He wanted possession and ownership, which he didn't have with his young friend because the boy could come and go whenever he wanted. There was only one way he could have what he wanted.

On October 4, 1988, Wes was released from probation. Wes had continued to molest Sammy when he was able to be alone with him. In April of 1989, Ralph, Ruth, and Sammy were given the opportunity to live in a larger home owned by their property manager. Wes continued living in the first home while the other three lived in the larger one. Wes preferred the privacy because he couldn't kidnap a child and bring him to his house if the others were with him.

There was a park close to Wes's house. One Saturday morning Wes could hear Sammy with his miniature Jeep playing with a girl in the park. Wes considered how he could get the two of them into his house and he would molest both of them. He would then send Sammy home and keep the girl through the weekend and kill her before he had to go to work on Monday. He would dig a deep grave on his property during the night and bury her there. He said he wanted her because he could get "real intercourse" with her. This full scenario came into his mind the few minutes he could hear Sammy and her playing. Fortunately, a woman came into the park, which kept it from happening.

There were other occasions when he would see children playing in the park. While watching them, he would develop elaborate scenarios in his mind of how he would get them in his house and molest and kill them. These scenarios were very detailed and covered multiple solutions to every possible problem that might occur.

Wes lived in the same house from the beginning of April 1989 until June or July of that same year. He lived only a few blocks from where he worked and he was friendly to everyone. People seemed to trust him. He never got the opportunity to get children into his house, other than

Sammy, who would come and visit him about three times a week. Wes soon moved into the larger house with Ralph and Ruth.

Around the middle of July, 1989, Cassie came back, but with a boyfriend and a young baby. She had been gone for over a year. Cassie, her boyfriend, and her baby moved in with Wes, Ralph, and Ruth, but within a week the boyfriend left. Cassie informed Wes she that wanted to be with him and she presented Wes with a four month old child named Bobby. She told Wes that this was his child, something Wes had sensed when he first saw the boy. She said she had left because she didn't feel she could tell him that she was pregnant.

Wes was ecstatic and again felt he had a chance to have a family. He agreed to renew the relationship, and again he gave up his plans for molesting and killing. As part of the deal, Wes agreed to allow Cassie's mother, Ruth, to live with them in the future.

Ralph was having alcohol problems at this time and things weren't working out between him and Ruth. Ruth considered leaving Ralph, and Cassie said that if she did, she wanted to go as well. Neither of them had any money coming in right then so Cassie approached Wes about going with them. She told Wes she loved him and wanted them to be a family, but Wes said he wanted them to stay where they were because he had a job with a fairly good income.

Wes never did have any influence over Cassie so when she said she was going with or without him, he agreed to go. Wes agreed to give up his job and relocate to Yakima ostensibly to allow Cassie and her mother to be around their friends. He didn't want to go but after he had been told that Bobby was his child he didn't want to lose him. Ralph evidently wasn't informed of this plan. Wes took what money he had, and he, Cassie's other two children left without informing Ralph.

When Cassie left him in Yakima and Wes was told he would never see his child, he became again, he was bitter and depressed. In Cassie's mind, Wes was merely a temporary relationship, and when the opportunity came to abandon him, she took it. Wes felt there was now only one direction for him to go. Back to children. This time he would follow through on his plan to turn them into sex slaves. During that week he made the contract with Satan to kidnap and kill children.

# Chapter 15

## David Douglas Park

Wes was desperately in need of comfort. His life was composed of two things, work and plans for sex with children. When he returned from his weeklong vacation with his father and stepmother he got a job and an apartment, but he was very lonely without children. Everybody around him appeared to be happy with their families and social activities. Wes had long ago given up believing he was part of the normal existence that everybody else shared. He was not like any of the kids he grew up with. He didn't have their popularity, their physical stature, or their socializing acumen. He was not part of their world. It was time to create his own world.

Friday, September 1st was a warm day at the David Douglas Park in Vancouver, Washington. The leaves on the trees were a deep rich green but a chill was entering into the night air, signaling the beginning to the end of summer. Westley Alan Dodd was new to the city but already he had become employed and had received his first paycheck, which he used to rent his own apartment. He normally would have taken some time to get acquainted with the local environment before looking for children to molest, but it was too late in the season for that luxury.

The David Douglas Park was a relatively large park with four baseball fields, playground equipment, a picnic area, and paved trails around its perimeter. It was situated in the middle of a residential area of the town which would generally have made it a bad choice for his activities. However, there were wooded areas 35 to 40 yards wide on the North and West sides of the park where he could hide a child while he carried out his act of violence. The trail through the park was about a mile long, and on the east end of the trail there was a marshy area complete with frogs—an attraction for little boys. On the southwest corner of the park there was a hill with scattered pieces of cardboard on it. The local kids used the cardboard as sleds to glide down the grassy hill. An ideal place to create trust in an unsuspecting child.

*Tell me about how you organized it.*

>I explored the park and I sketched a thorough diagram of it, including directions of the trails,

> distances from one trail to another and from one location to another. I marked where I would park my car and I put an x at the best strategic location where I could sit and observe the movements of the children coming into the park. I would rather have brought a kid to my apartment but I hadn't lived there long enough observe my landlady's routines. She might see me with the child and she would tell the police of it when she saw the boy's picture in the paper. I concluded that I'd have to stay in the park and simply molest and murder right there.

Over the years, Wes had visualized the monster, then pretended to be the monster, and now had become the monster. He would make a complete and detailed account of his plans prior to the killing and he would log the details both before and after. He couldn't think of anyone who had kept a scientific journal about committing murder, except for Dr. Frankenstein in the movie. But in that movie the good doctor wanted to create life. The life Wes planned to create was his own but he would have to destroy the life of a child in order to do it. He didn't understand that to have a child die at his hand was to bond the image and memory of the child to him forever, and that it would begin his own psychic death. It would be the inception of the final phase of an insidious evil process that would initiate a rapid downhill descent to his own execution.

> I put these thoughts on paper, wanting to document everything—it would help me to remem-

ber and fantasize later, and it would be useful to analyze for signs of danger spots, mistakes, and it would be used in writing my book about my experiences. If I were to die in a car wreck or something, my logs would be found, and at least the parents would know what happened to their kids.

# Chapter 16

## The Plan

Wes began his preparations for the crime by logging the date and time he would leave his apartment. He would go to the park for his stakeout with his murder kit which consisted of a three foot cord wrapped around his waist, hidden by his shirt; a six inch fillet knife in a sheath inside his right sock; and an ace bandage wrapped around the lower part of his leg which could be used as a gag or to could keep the knife from falling out if he had to run.

Once he had determined that everything was in place and at the precise moment listed in his log, he headed back to the park.

There were no opportunities that presented themselves on Saturday, or on Sunday. Either the children were with their parents or siblings or they were too old. Children who had reached puberty were not as acceptable because they were more difficult to control.

**Monday, September 4, 1989**

On Monday, Wes positioned himself at a point where a side trail broke off from the main trail and curved back to a marshy area. Four girls ages about four to eight approached him, leading a boy who was about two years old. He had watched them come out of the apartments across the street from the parking lot and felt an adrenaline rush as they came into the park towards him. He wanted the boy and he decided that this would be his chance.

As they approached him, Wes quickly rehearsed the scenario he would use: "Hey, would you kids like to see some baby birds that I just found? They're down that way. I can show you but it's best that I take only one of you at a time so we don't frighten them too much." He would take the one child back into the woods and kill her, then come back for the second child. Lastly, he would take the remaining girl and the boy back to the same area. He would kill the girl and then take the boy to his apartment—in spite of his concerns about his landlady.

As the group got closer he could hear the oldest girl telling the others that they shouldn't go down into the darker part of the trail (where Wes was sitting) because they might be kidnapped by some killer. One of the girls pointed to Wes and said, "What about him?"

Wes wondered if they could sense something. Perhaps they could detect danger like he could sense a child's vulnerability. He hesitated approaching them. They took another trail. Away from him. Away from danger.

A little later five boys came into the park. There were too many and they looked a little too old but he was past the point of caring about how many there were or their ages. Again, he rehearsed in his mind his divide-and-conquer strategy, but this time he would invite them to see a snake he had found instead of baby birds. Boys were more interested in snakes. But the boys turned and went out into an open field before he could get to them.

Later he saw two women with two girls and a boy on the hill where he had seen the cardboard sleds. He hoped they would let the boy stay there and play by himself as they went somewhere else in the park. They didn't.

Wes had begun walking east along the main trail when he heard someone approaching from behind. A boy of about 10 pushed his bike past Wes. He had on red sweat pants which fit tightly to his body. Wes's heart raced wildly as he moved quickly to catch up with the fast moving boy. He would use the snake routine and would get the kid to bring his bike back into the deeper woods where it wouldn't be seen.

He caught up to the boy and was just about to start his routine when he heard someone behind him. He turned and saw the boy's father on a bike. Wes turned off the trail, angry and frustrated. There were effective techniques and ineffective techniques, and Wes knew he had the best well-thought-out and well-practiced plan but he hadn't been given the chance to set it into play.

It was almost noon. He returned to his apartment, wrote a detailed account in his log of everything that had happened that morning and then made a sandwich. He returned to the park at 4:00 pm. He figured he had one more hour before it would start to get dark and all the kids would go home. "It was now or never." He was prepared to approach as many as five kids in a group as long as there were no adults and no teenagers and he didn't care if the victim he molested was a boy or a girl.

For added confidence, he reflected back on the detailed plans he had outlined in his journal. It was to be his instruction manual, set into print, and it would be modified if necessary depending on how it worked out tonight. He would eventually have a how-to book, a guide for killing children.

> Having written things down and planned gave me confidence. I'd never done this before. It was as if I were writing then studying an instruction manual. Writing helped to visualize possible circumstances or situations that may arise, and I had something tangible to look at and analyze for weaknesses in my plans. It was also exciting! Fantasies were okay, but putting it all on paper made it more exciting. By writing it, the fantasies were more life-like and lasted longer.

# Chapter 17

## The Neer Brothers

He returned to the park and while walking west along a path closest to the woods he saw two boys, one by his bike and the other preparing to roll down a hill. One boy appeared at the upper level of his acceptable age limit and the other was even older. They weren't his ideal targets but it was getting late and he didn't want to pass up this opportunity.

He considered his options but there was no time to use the snake routine. He would simply tell them to come with him. If they did he would know he had them. If they didn't, he would quickly leave the park hoping they couldn't give an accurate description to the police, and he would try somewhere else next weekend.

I walked up to the older of the two boys, and said in an authoritative voice, "I want you two to come with me." The one boy asked why. I said "Just come with me and you'll find out. Bring your bikes with you so no one will steal them before we're done."

The boys picked up their bikes and followed him west along the trail towards Andresan Road. The younger of the two kept up a running conversation, "Do you want us to help you look for something? Do you want to show us something?" Wes simply said, "You'll see." The boys trusted him, believing they were about to do something fun or see something interesting.

Wes asked them their names and their ages: Cole Neer, age 11, and his brother Billy, age 10. It wasn't how he had planned it, but it would do. He would record this change of strategy in his log and he would emphasize that a strong but kind command turned out to be as effective as he had thought the baby birds or snake approach would be.

Part way up the trail they passed two older boys who were on a parallel path to the side of them. Wes told them, "I don't want you guys talking to anyone." They didn't, but he noticed they were becoming nervous.

A quarter mile further down the path he led them off into a deeper wooded area. Their bikes were left a short distance from the trail where they would be hidden from the eyes of those who might wonder the whereabouts of their owners. He continued southeast for a short distance and found a spot concealed by bushes and a large tree about 25 feet from the trail.

Wes said, "This looks like a good place for it." He was toying with them. He knew what the "it" was. They didn't. He wanted to offer his victims a slight peek at the up and coming event which was playing over and over again in his mind. He wanted to see how long he could play with their minds without them suspecting danger. However, there wasn't the time for that, even though it would reflect his brilliance, his superiority, and his exceptional skills at cunning and subterfuge. Perhaps another time.

He told the boys that he was going to play a game with them. He got them to sit on the ground with their backs to each other. He tied their hands together and then began to molest them, starting with Cole, then Billy. It bothered him that he couldn't get sexually aroused. He began stabbing the boys. Billy was able to get loose and started running towards the path in an attempt to get away. He had gotten within five feet of the path when Wes caught up to him. As he grabbed the boy, Billy yelled out, "I'm sorry, I'm sorry."

> When I pulled the knife out of my sock I went blank. I had an unbelievable adrenaline rush. Anxiety maybe. It was not like my fantasies. I just went on automatic and got it done.

# Chapter 18

## The Escape

*What did you do next?*

I ran back towards the park entrance where I had parked my car. At first I was confused about the direction. I forced myself to slow down because if somebody saw me running they would tell the police when they found the bodies of the boys. I realized I was still holding the bloody knife in my hand. I wiped it off and put it back in its sheath. I had panicked and I had run away too fast. I turned around and walked back to where I had left the boys to make sure I hadn't left any evidence. Both boys seemed dead.

I then started back on the path, said hello to an elderly couple coming into the park, threw a softball back to a group of boys playing ball, got into my car, and drove back to my apartment. I wrote about the event in my diary, took a shower, and drove over to my father's place. I didn't want to have to think about what I had done.

*But if this was something you had been planning, something you were excited about carrying off, what was it you didn't want to think about?*

What was it I didn't want to think about when I went to Dad's after the murder of the two boys? I don't know. Part of the reason for going was to try to establish an alibi, should the need arise. I didn't know how to feel, and I had more adrenalin than blood flowing in my veins. I wanted to try to do something "normal" and try to calm down, rather than think about what I'd done and possibly do something to give myself away. I just needed to completely step out of the picture—not wanting to think too much about it until I could calm down and figure out what I was feeling when I got a grip on myself. I was on an adrenalin rush, and was afraid of being reckless or careless and making mistakes. I had to stop thinking about it until I could be more careful and aware, and avoid mistakes that could lead to my arrest.

I really don't remember any of my actual feelings that night, but the next day I was in a state of disbelief: I can't believe I really did it. I really did what I planned. I raped and killed a child—two boys. But I was scared—afraid I'd left behind a clue for police and I'd be caught. That scared feeling blocked out anything else I may have been feeling. But then again it was a new experience and I didn't know how to feel.

When the scared feeling started to leave I started wishing I'd done more before killing them, and that I had taken more time to look at the older boy's body, and I decided I'd have to bring the next one home to have more time for those things. I do remember covering up the guilt, and when I felt guilty I'd tell myself how much fun the next one would be. I listened to a news broadcast the next morning and I heard that one of the boys was still alive. For a moment I hoped the boy would live but then I realized that if he did, he could identify me.

The boy died. Wes felt some regret over what he had done and it bothered him that he didn't have a full memory of the homicides. He was particularly bothered by the memory of Billy saying he was sorry. Wes was haunted by this voice. When I talked to him in prison, he got tears in his eyes when I brought it up.

# Chapter 19

## Lee Islie

On October 28th Wes drove to Portland, Oregon and selected another park with a wooded area surrounding it. He watched for a victim all that Saturday but a suitable opportunity didn't present itself. The following day, he kidnapped a boy named Lee who was playing on a swing set while his brother watched some boys playing ball.

This boy was to be Wes's downfall. Lee was a substitute for Sammy and for his son Bobby. Wes took Lee to his apartment and tried to make friends with him. Later in the evening, he took Lee to a store and bought him a toy with the boy's promise that by doing so Lee would spend the night with him. Wes then took him to McDonald's, and they went inside to eat. Since the boy had been cooperative and trusting with him, he felt the boy wouldn't cry out or try to run away.

Wes was doing everything he could to make friends with the boy. He didn't want him to be frightened. He allowed him to play on the playground equipment at McDonald's with a young girl while Wes talked to the girl's father. He felt totally confident that the boy wouldn't try to run from him, and he didn't.

Wes was now having mixed feelings about the boy. He had molested Lee once and had planned on doing so again during the night, but he couldn't get sexually aroused. He felt compassion for the boy and it hurt him when the boy cried. He couldn't stand to see the boy cry. He felt close to the boy as he slept next to him that night and he didn't want to end his life the next morning. He had to go to work. He couldn't leave the boy alone yet he didn't want to let him go. He killed the boy and, in an attempt to hide him should his landlady come into his apartment while he was at work, he strapped a rope around the boy's body and hung him in the closet.

# Chapter 20

## The Aftermath of Lee's Death

*Wes, you had killed three boys and you were considering killing others. Did you become more cautious or were you willing to take more chances?*

After the murder (of Lee) I was *definitely* a master criminal who had committed a perfect crime, and felt I could get away with *anything*. I was even considering toying with police. Had I got the next boy home I was considering writing on his body "Billy and Cole were number 1 & 2. Lee was number 3. Here's number 4. Who and where is number 5?" or something similar. The police did not believe the murders were connected, so I wanted to tie them together thus showing the stupidity of the police to assume they weren't connected, and also let them know there would be more murders, and that I didn't think they could catch me.

They had no clues, no motive—I'd committed the *perfect* crime, and wanted to rub it in. Had it not been for my diary and the pictures I took of Lee, they never could have connected me to the murders. Those items plus my confession is all the prosecutor had, and I would not have confessed if the diary and pictures didn't exist.

I would have laughed at getting away with the murders. so after the last murder I felt like the master criminal. And I felt nothing for the kids. Had I got that 4$^{th}$ boy home he'd have been gagged, raped, and tortured in any number of ways, depending on whether or not the neighbors were home, and I would not have given his cries and screams a second thought.

*Did you not feel guilt at all?*

Yeah, I did, but it didn't last long. I would start feeling sorry for what I did to those kids, then I'd suddenly realize that I was fantasizing about what I would do to the next kid. I would start feeling guilty and *automatically* block out those feelings by fantasizing about the next one, and it would happen before I realized it.

Wes tried to avoid guilt through narcissistic self-aggrandizement. He couldn't allow himself to believe that he

## The Case of Westley Allan Dodd

had done something horribly wrong; his only option was to idealize his pathology. The more Wes began to feel badly for what he had done, the more he attempted to artificially elevate himself in his own eyes so that he didn't see what he had done—or what he had become. Wes had to find something positive in his evil and he attempted to do so by believing that someone so formidable as him couldn't be bad. He elevated himself in his own mind to an exalted level of power and he assumed the role of God. He could now take and give life as God did and he could become as powerful and as omnipotent as God.

A professional criminal is cautious and respectful of the police. A person who is desperately trying to convince himself that he is something he knows he is not may thrust the pretense into the realm of extreme exaggeration.

> I knew without a doubt that I could bring a child home and do whatever I damn well pleased, because no one would know, and I'd never become suspect. I was no longer afraid of ever being caught. There was nothing left to prevent me from carrying out even the worst of my rape/torture/mutilation slow, painful death fantasies. I could even play games with police. I was invulnerable. All I could do was laugh at the police and think how smart I was, and what a great planner I was.
> 
> They'd treat me like a god—always respecting my power over their lives. They'd be almost in a po-

sition of having to worship me to stay alive. Being able to kill at will gave me absolute control.

Wes planned on finding and kidnapping his son Bobby. He said he would play the role of God and his own son Bobby would become Jesus.

> I would tell my sex slaves how great my son was which would make them angry at me and my son Bobby—angry enough to make them kill my own son. I would tell them someone had to die, and my only son's death would save their lives. I was going to mock what God did by sending Jesus to die, and let my slaves know that even my own son was not beyond being killed with my permission. If I would allow them to kill my only son, they must bow down to my every desire. I guess at work I was afraid to give orders to the people I hired, but I was going to make up for that by acting like God at home.

# Chapter 21

## The Capture

Wes was now experiencing a deep sense of loneliness. He had murdered three boys but this hadn't brought him any satisfaction. It was an empty victory. He no longer had access to Sammy or Bobby or any of the other children he had molested. He was still alone. He could decide to change his life. He could perhaps just molest children and not kill any more. No, that wouldn't work because he would get reported and be sent to prison. He couldn't give up on molesting children because to him there was no relationship without sex. Children were his only friends. They were the only ones that truly cared for him—at least in his fantasies.

He had been a child molester for so long he didn't know how to be anything else. If he didn't think about children what would there be to think about? The only option that he could see was to continue on the course he had chosen for himself. He couldn't allow himself to consider other options because there were none. He had to rise to the occasion. He had to believe he was right. He had to become the master criminal.

A short time later, Wes went into a theater in an attempt to abduct a child. While taking the child out of the theater the boy screamed and struggled against him and Wes had to let him go. He didn't get caught.

A short time after that, Wes tried to do the same thing from another theater in an adjoining town. Again, the child struggled and was able to get away. Wes left the crime scene in his vehicle, but he said it broke down a few blocks away. The police caught him, and while interrogating him for the attempted abductions, Wes reported that one of the officers said to him, "Wes, if you were us what would you do?" Wes reportedly said, "If I were you I would search my apartment." At this point, realizing what he had said, he confessed to the three homicides.

Wes chose not to appeal for his life. He wanted to die. He was executed by hanging on January 5th, 1993 at the Washington State Penitentiary. He selected hanging because, "I don't think I deserve a nice easy death. I don't deserve something better than what those boys got."

Wes was later to confide that after being arrested he plead with God for forgiveness. The last time I saw Wes was one week before his execution. At times there were tears in his eyes when he talked about the dark side within him and about Billy's haunting voice saying, "I'm sorry, I'm sorry." However, he freely admitted that if he were ever to be released from prison he would probably continue killing children. Instead, his last act of destruction was be to bring about his own annihilation.

Could something have been done to have kept Wes from killing those three children? Probably. There were many signs throughout his life that something was wrong. Laws have been changed so that a person can't be a repeat offender and avoid the consequences as easily as Wes did. However, maybe it's time that we put added emphasis on understanding and helping children during their formative years.

# Appendix A

Wes wrote a pamphlet when he was in prison called, "When You Meet a Stranger or Other Bad People." He had copies made and distributed to anyone who wanted one. The following is a transcript of that pamphlet.

## What Is A Stranger? Who Are Bad People?

My name is Wes, but since you don't really know me, I am a stranger to you. I am the kind of stranger you should stay away from. There are other people like me. We make you pull your pants down or take your clothes off. Some of us make you get in our cars, or try to trick you so you'll get in our cars. We can be nice to you, and maybe give you money or play games with you, or we might be very mean. When we are nice, it is so we can trick you into doing something bad.

Sometimes, some of us want to hurt, or even kill you.

A stranger can be a man or woman, but sometimes the person who wants to do bad things to you is someone you know. It could be your neighbor, a babysitter, or an older friend. It could even be another kid the same age as you. It might be a cousin, aunt or uncle, or even someone in your own family. It could be *anyone*.

People you know and love might try to see or touch your private parts. A stranger might try to do something even worse. It doesn't matter *what* we want to do to you. You don't have to let us do what we want to you. You *can* get away from us. How?

Sometimes the person that wants to do bad things is scared, too! The person is afraid you will do something to get him (or her) caught. How can *you* make a stranger or other person leave you alone?

## What do you do?
### Just Say NO!

You may have heard "just say no" to drugs. You can also say NO to someone that tells you to pull down your pants or take your clothes off.

One day I met a boy playing in a park. I said hi and asked what his name was. I pretended to be a nice person and told him I knew a better place to play, so he went with me to a different part of the park where there were lots of trees. When we got to a place where no one else could see us, I told him to pull his pants down. I touched his private parts with my hands and mouth.

I met another boy at the same park. When I told him to pull his pants down, he said NO! I said he couldn't leave until he did it. He said "NO! I'm not doing it!" I told him he could go—he didn't have to pull his pants down.

Why did the first boy have to pull his pants down, but not the second boy? Because the second boy said NO! Nothing bad happened to the second boy.

### RUN!

Sometimes, just saying no doesn't work. One boy kept telling me no, but I wouldn't let him go. He finally let me do what I wanted to him so I would go away. *You* don't have to give up like he did. You can still get away. Do you know how?

One day a little girl told me no. Then, before I could make her pull her pants down anyway, she ran away! I was afraid someone would see me chasing her and might take me to the police, so I let her go. She said no and ran away, so nothing bad happened to her.

### SCREAM! YELL!

What happens if you say no, but the person holds you so you can't run, or catches you before you get to a safe place? Do you let the person do what he (or she) wants, and hope it doesn't hurt? NO!

One boy said no and tried to run, but I grabbed his arm and wouldn't let him go. He couldn't get away so I pulled his pants down. Is there anything else he could have done to protect himself? What?

I found a 6 year old boy and told him, "You have to come with me." He said NO and tried to get away from me, but I picked him and up and started to carry him away. He knew he couldn't get away, but he didn't give up. He started screaming and yelled, "Someone help me—he's killing me!" I told him to be quiet, but he kept yelling for help. I was afraid someone would hear him, so I let him go and [he] ran away.

When I let him go he did a very good thing. He *ran* and *told someone* what happened, and the police were able to catch me. I am in prison now and can never try to hurt any more boys and girls.

That 6 year old boy didn't know what I was going to do. He only knew I was trying to take him away and something real bad could happen. He's a hero now, because even though he was afraid of me, he screamed and *yelled for help* when he needed it. He's also a hero because *he told someone right away* so the police could catch me.

## BE A HERO!

If that 6-year-old boy can be a hero, so can you! When *you* meet a stranger that wants you to go with him (or her), or when *anyone* wants you to pull down your pants or do something else you know is bad, *Just say NO!* Then *RUN! SCREAM*—it will scare him [or her] away! *YELL* for *HELP!* Get away fast and tell someone what happened! *Always* tell someone!

Sometimes the person will leave you alone if you say you'll tell on them. Then tell someone as soon as you can. If they won't leave you alone, get away. Run to the closest safe place you know of. Run to your house. If the person is at your house, run to the neighbor's house.

Find an adult that will help you. If you can't find help, find a phone. Call 9-1-1. Even if you don't know where you are, stay on the phone. If you stay on the phone the police will be able to find you and help you. You *can* do it! Be a hero!

## Is It Too Late?

Has something bad already happened to you or someone you know? If it did, *please tell someone*. Tell your mom and dad, or your teacher. Tell someone you trust.

The person doing bad things might tell you it's a secret or make you promise not to tell, or the person might say he'll hurt you or someone you love if you tell. Tell on the person anyway. The person won't hurt you or anyone else—that's just a trick so you won't tell on him and he won't get caught. If he doesn't get caught, he (or she) can do it again.

If something bad happens to you, it's not your fault. It's OK to tell someone. They can help you and you'll feel

# The Case of Westley Allan Dodd

better. They can make sure it doesn't happen to you again. Even if the person doing bad things is someone you love, tell somebody else what happened. You'll love each other even more when the bad things stop!

I'm glad that 6-year-old boy told on me. now I can never do bad things to any more boys or girls. What do you do when someone wants to do bad things to you? Just say *NO! RUN! SCREAM! YELL! GET AWAY! TELL SOMEONE!* You *can* protect yourself and other kids too! Be a hero!

# Part Three: Comparison Between Arthur Gary Bishop and Westley Alan Dodd

Dodd and Bishop were loners. When Dodd got a bicycle he spent lengthy periods of time away from home exploring alone. Bishop always had a desire to be like the other boys so he would try to copy their behavior. Neither of them fit in. That is, neither of them was liked well enough to have other kids seek their companionship. Dodd and Bishop shared feelings of deep humiliation imposed on them by their peers. Kids made fun of Dodd in the locker room and in school. Dodd was extremely bothered by this but he didn't have anyone he felt he could talk to about it. Bishop was teased because he was overweight, wore glasses and had a mild speech impediment. They wanted to be like the other kids, but each felt inferior to their peers, and responded by being passive.

Dodd had all the toys he wanted as a child. He had cousins he could play with and enjoyed doing so, but he never felt that he was an integral part of the family. He was the first child and his father told him that when the second child was born (his brother), he withdrew into a corner and never came out. Bishop had a fairly normal childhood in that he had siblings, parents, and grandparents who were always part of the family structure.

Neither Dodd nor Bishop indicated they could confide in their parents about life issues such as friends, activities or problems.

Their parents, teachers, and other adults saw them as "nice kids" by. The other kids avoided them, for the most part. This generated loneliness in them and caused them to seek gratification in solitary pursuits. The "nice boy" image they displayed prevented others from seeing what was taking place on the inside. In each case, people were shocked and in disbelief when Dodd and Bishop were arrested for killing children.

Nether Dodd nor Bishop had any learning problems in elementary school. They performed fairly well academically in high school. Bishop went to college. Dodd was offered the chance for a scholarship to college to major in music.

Both Dodd and Bishop got heavily involved in reading fantasy. It was an escape from the unhappy reality of their lives. Both said that when they stopped reading, they could put the book down but they couldn't stop the fantasy that continued in their mind. Fantasy in and of itself was not the problem. The problem was that it became their primary means of gratification. Neither of them became involved in sports or other school or social activities. Fantasy took the place of relationships. It was a substitute for family and friends.

Dodd and Bishop both had an early interest in sex.

For both of them, when they reached puberty and discovered masturbation, the excitement and relief from loneliness and stress was so strong and intense that they felt this discovery was the most exciting and important thing that had ever happened to them.

Neither Dodd nor Bishop used drugs and, for the most part, not alcohol either. Bishop tried alcohol a couple of times but didn't want to become addicted to it so he gave it up.

Both had negative experiences with girls early in their lives. They both found children to be more approachable. They believed that girls avoided them but children were accepting and trusting. It's unclear if either of them could have had a normal relationship with a girl their age when they were in junior high or high school. When Bishop was young he asked a girl to be his girlfriend but was rejected by her. When Dodd met Cassie he was ecstatic that he had found a girlfriend and he threw his pictures of children in the trash. He enjoyed sex with her.

Both Dodd and Bishop were arrested in their teens: Dodd for exposing himself to children and Bishop for shoplifting. Both completed probation.

## A Comparison of Bishop and Dodd

Westley Dodd's first major turning point in his life was when he did his exploratory and sexual activities at the pond. His second major turning point was when he exposed himself from the upstairs window of his home to children returning from elementary school. In both cases he felt that he wouldn't get into trouble and, for the most part, he didn't. His sexual activities continued after that. He became extremely confident in himself and became narcissistic. By the time Dodd was 15 years old, sex with children was his primary goal for his future.

Art Bishop's primary turning point was when he was on his religious mission for his church. He had been fighting his sexual temptations for years but when he found himself in a foreign country with many young, nude boys running around, he felt that he would never be able to control his sexual interest in children. He gave up on God and on himself. However, I believe that he wasn't completely unsatisfied with his decision to give up God. He anticipated that sexual satisfaction would be a daily enjoyable activity while rewards from God were viewed as distant and uncertain.

Dodd reported no bouts of severe depression. However, he likely had some when his peers at school rejected him. Bishop reported only one deep depression, which was when he was on his religious mission and felt that he had disappointed God by committing an unpardonable sin.

As adults, both Dodd and Bishop were arrested and charged with a felony, Dodd on a sex charge and Bishop for embezzlement. They were each required to go to therapy. Dodd wouldn't talk to his first therapist about his problems because it was the same therapist his father was going to. Even when he did have a therapist of his own, he seemed open and cooperative admitted to some of his crimes. However, he only reported part of his crimes and he was narcissistically proud of himself that he could withhold information from his therapist. Bishop also *appeared* to be open and cooperative, but it was only about his embezzlement. I don't believe that either wanted to take a chance of possibly being cured of an addiction they didn't want to give up. Arthur Bishop also said the problem was that therapy would take something from him but not give him something to put in its place.

Dodd didn't seem to mind being in jail for a sex crime. Bishop was terrified of how other inmates would treat him if they knew he was a child molester. Both Dodd and Bishop were determined to not lose their freedom again. This set them up for homicide.

Dodd decided he would have to kill a victim in order to keep the child from talking to the police. He had one failed attempt of homicide at a construction site and told himself that he would have to plan it much better the next time. Bishop had no intent to kill a child but when he could see that it was either that or to go to prison, he didn't hesitate in doing so.

Dodd's first homicide was extremely well planned. Bishop's first homicide was an impulsive response to the fear of going to prison.

During their first homicides, each felt a detachment, a type of dissociation. After their first homicide, each had

## A Comparison of Bishop and Dodd

difficulty being alone but soon got over this. Neither had any difficulty with the thought of killing another child. Both experienced brief regret following their first homicide but neither said they experienced any lasting guilt afterwards. Both said that when they did feel some regret they would quickly put those thoughts out of their minds and replace them with sexual thoughts.

Because of the tenuous nature of a relationship between an adult and a boy, both had a strong fear of a boy leaving them. Neither Dodd nor Bishop had the capacity for empathy. They either never had it or they lost it early in their lives. They had no concern about how they were damaging a boy's life. They were both psychopathically self-centered.

Both Dodd and Bishop created a system of justification for their behavior. Dodd viewed himself as a scientist conducting medical experiments. He would keep a journal with details of these experiments in his vehicle so that if he got killed in an accident someone would find the journal and the parents of his victims would hopefully get some closure by knowing what had happened to their child.

Bishop justified it in the following way:

> First, I had already broken a tremendously significant taboo by killing Alonzo [his first victim]. My feelings and emotions after his death were ambivalent. At times I felt empty and dammed by what I had done, but at other times I was disappointed in his death because the events associated with it were fading from my memory and becom-

ing unreal. I didn't get any pleasure from the act of killing Alonzo, but I did derive sexual satisfaction before and after his death. As my recollection of his death grew dimmer, so did my sexual pleasure from the memory. I felt sad because it seemed somehow to make Alonzo's death less meaningful and significant. And that made his death unacceptable to me. It was as if I agreed with another part of my mind which insisted that next time things will be done to make the murder more memorable. Therefore, murder was maintained as an acceptable act, at least in my mind.

Second, because I had killed before, it was much easier to kill again. Much of the stigma and revulsion attached to murder were now gone, and a subconscious sense of "you can only go to Hell once" again made the thought of additional murder acceptable to me, especially when I considered only the possible pleasure promised by the sexual activity before and after.

With both Dodd and Bishop, there was a growing sense of dissatisfaction in what they were doing. Both said they handled their feelings of regret by pushing the thoughts about their crimes out of their heads and replacing them with sexual thoughts about their victims.

Both Dodd and Bishop were very lonely and they viewed relationships with children as their primary source

## A Comparison of Bishop and Dodd

of happiness. To each, a child was a friend, a son, a lover, a companion, and a replacement for their family.

Both had a problem when it came to the second opportunity to kidnap a victim. Neither had anything against finding another victim but in both instances the experience was different from what they had anticipated. Bishop's second homicide was fairly easy for him, but it was empty of any excitement. Dodd had a much more difficult time with his second homicide because he saw the boy as a substitute son. He took the boy to McDonald's and bought him something to eat inside the restaurant. He let the boy play in the recreational area with another child while he chatted with her father. He enjoyed playing the role of a father with his son. He didn't want to take the life of the boy but he felt he had no choice because he had to go to work the next morning.

In both cases, as time went on, their lives and their emotions deteriorated and they became desperate. Neither knew how to fix things so both felt they had to kidnap and kill other children. Dodd had an unrealistic plan of having sex slaves who would be under his control.

When each was picked up by the police and were interrogated, both admitted guilt without asking for an attorney, and both confessed to the homicides of all the children they had murdered, not just the one case the police were investigating.

When they were given death sentences by the court, both petitioned for an early execution. Both said they didn't want to go on killing children, but if they were ever free to do so, the desire to molest children was so strong they wouldn't be able to stop. Both told me they didn't understand how or why they had become that way.

Of particular interest, both Westley Alan Dodd and Arthur Gary Bishop deteriorated fairly rapidly in their emotional control and behavior as they continued their quest to find new victims. Considering how the police caught them, it would appear that each had set himself up to be caught, yet both told me they had no intention of wanting the police to apprehend them.

The sexual activity wasn't giving them what they were looking for. Wes got very emotionally close to two boys, and he lost both of them. Art had the same experience. Family, friends, cousins, grandparents, and social activities were out of the picture. Both were very desperate to have someone in their lives, but both knew it could never happen voluntarily. Wes decided the only way he could ward off his loneliness was to have sex slaves, and he justified it by saying he would conduct medical experiments for science and he would keep a record of his findings. However, I believe he had created a fantasy and he was trying, against all odds, to keep it alive.

Art "bought" his companions. He embezzled from work, well over $40,000. He had been caught once and undoubtedly realized that he wouldn't be able to get away with it forever no matter how many companies he worked for. He got tired of having to change residences and identifications. Without embezzling money he would never have the funds to keep his companions interested in him.

# A Comparison of Bishop and Dodd

Both were extremely addicted to sex with boys and both felt that life had no meaning unless there were children in the picture.

With both of them, the primary sexual activities, at least in the beginning, were self-stimulating fantasy activities.

There was no chance for peace in their lives.

For either of them.

# Conclusion

Arthur Gary Bishop and Westley Alan Dodd are both dead. Both, by their own requests, have been executed.

What did we gain by their deaths? We got justice. We don't have to see their faces or hear their stories as we would have had they stretched out their appeals for several years. We know that they will never be able to harm children again. We hope that potential child molesters will learn from their examples and curb their desires and leave children alone. However, we still frequently hear about attempts at kidnapping children, and there are no signs that our children will be any safer in the future.

We have had to learn to caution our children not to talk to strangers. Gone are the days when a man who has

# The Case of Arthur Gary Bishop

an extra lollipop can offer it to a child sitting in a park swing. But until we can get child molesters off the streets this will be a necessary precaution in an attempt to keep our children safe.

In crime thrillers, the bad guy gets caught, the hero rides off into the sunset, and everybody feels safe and happy again. It's clear and simple. When Dodd and Bishop were executed, some people felt that society was safer with them dead. However, it isn't as clear and simple as we would like it to be. Executing these killers doesn't fully resolve the problem. If we can better understand how little children can grow to become monsters it will at least be a step in the right direction. Bluntly put, it's difficult to change what we don't understand.

# Acknowledgments

When I was employed as a psychologist at the Utah State Prison I had the opportunity to engage in research on violent inmates. The projects initially began when I completed a psychological assessment on Ted Bundy for the court. Soon after that Arthur Gary Bishop, who had murdered five children in Salt Lake City, asked me to help him understand how and why he could take the lives of innocent children since he professed a strong love for children. I was initially surprised that he didn't know but I soon came to realize that he really didn't understand the process of how it happened. Other criminals such as Westley Alan Dodd, Keith Jesperson, Piere Selby, as well as a Vietnam

War veteran who became a contract killer and a number of others volunteered for my research. I owe thanks to each these people for sharing their lives in order to help me understand the development of the violent mind.

Special appreciation goes to my agent, Carrie Anne Keller, who first suggested that I put into print the findings of my research. I owe thanks to my publisher Steven W. Booth and my editor Leya Booth for suggesting that we do a series of books on these offenders entitled *The Development of the Violent Mind*. Without their patience and encouragement this project would not have been completed. I am very grateful to Dr. Michael R. Collings for his editorial consultation as well as his positive inspiration.

Special thanks to Carol Rogers, a colleague of mine, who gave me valuable feedback on the Westley Dodd manuscript.

Special thanks also goes to Shelley Welsh in Nova Scotia. In spite of her busy schedule with her employment she has been willing to take the time to read my manuscripts and provide me with valuable feedback. Her interest in helping me to be a better writer is greatly appreciated.

Made in the USA
Lexington, KY
13 March 2018